GOD'S POWER
for
FATHERS

God's Power For Fathers

Published By:
C&D International
9029 Directors Row
Dallas, Texas 75247
Telephone: (214) 638-5668

ISBN: 0-937347-76-0

ACKNOWLEDGEMENTS

God has called each Christian father to be the spiritual leader of his home. It is our prayer that this book will provide each father with a scriptural guide to achieve this goal.

We are deeply indebted to Robert C. Larson for his endless research in the development of this book and we at C &D International feel honored to have the privilege of providing this material as a spiritual guide to all fathers.

Contents

13. God's Dynamic Examples Of Fathers Who Cared... • 265

God Freely Gives You...

Eternal hope for your family

Sing unto the Lord with thanksgiving; sing praise upon the harp unto our God:

Who covereth the heaven with clouds, who prepareth rain for the earth, who maketh grass to grow upon the mountains.

He giveth to the beast his food, and to the young ravens which cry.

He delighteth not in the strength of the horse: he taketh not pleasure in the legs of a man.

The Lord taketh pleasure in them that fear him, in those that hope in his mercy.

Praise the Lord, O Jerusalem; praise thy God, O Zion.

For he hath strengthened the bars of thy gates; he hath blessed thy children within thee.

Psalms 147:7-13

But let us, who are of the day, be sober, putting on the breastplate of faith and love; and for an helmet, the hope of salvation.

For God hath not appointed us to wrath, but to obtain salvation by our Lord Jesus Christ,

Who died for us, that, whether we wake or sleep, we should live together with him.

Wherefore comfort yourselves together, and edify one another, even as also ye do.

I Thessalonians 5:8-11

But God, who is rich in mercy, for his great love wherewith he loved us,

Even when we were dead in sins, hath quickened us together with Christ, (by grace ye are saved;)

And hath raised us up together, and made us sit together in heavenly places in Christ Jesus:

That in the ages to come he might shew the exceeding riches of his grace in his kindness toward us through Christ Jesus.

Ephesians 2:4-7

If ye then be risen with Christ, seek those things which are above, where Christ sitteth on the right hand of God.

Set your affection on things above, not on things on the earth.

For ye are dead, and your life is hid with Christ in God.

When Christ, who is our life, shall appear, then shall ye also appear with him in glory.

Colossians 3:1-4

For the hope which is laid up for you in heaven, whereof ye heard before in the word of the truth of the gospel;

Which is come unto you, as it is in all the world; and bringeth forth fruit, as it doth also in you, since the day ye heard of it, and knew the grace of God in truth:

Colossians 1:5, 6

Knowing that a man is not justified by the works of the law, but by the faith of Jesus Christ, even we have believed in Jesus Christ, that we might be justified by the faith of Christ, and not by the works of the law: for by the works of the law shall no flesh be justified.

I am crucified with Christ: nevertheless I live; yet not I, but Christ liveth in me: and the life which I now live in the flesh I live by the faith of the Son of God, who loved me, and gave himself for me.

Galatians 2:16, 20

Let that therefore abide in you, which ye have heard from the beginning. If that which ye have heard from the beginning shall remain in you, ye also shall continue in the Son, and in the Father.

And this is the promise that he hath promised us, even eternal life.

I John 2:24, 25

For the wages of sin is death; but the gift of God is eternal life through Jesus Christ our Lord.

Romans 6:23

For as many as are led by the Spirit of God, they are the sons of God.

For ye have not received the spirit of bondage again to fear; but ye have received the Spirit of adoption, whereby we cry, Abba, Father.

The Spirit itself beareth witness with our spirit, that we are the children of God:

And if children, then heirs; heirs of God, and joint-heirs with Christ; if so be that we suffer with him, that we may be also glorified together.

For I reckon that the sufferings of this present time are not worthy to be compared with the glory which shall be revealed in us.

For we are saved by hope: but hope that is seen is not hope: for what a man seeth, why doth he yet hope for?

But if we hope for that we see not, then do we with patience wait for it.

Romans 8:14-18, 24, 25

Blessed be the God and Father of our Lord Jesus Christ, which according to his abundant mercy hath begotten us again unto a lively hope by the resurrection of Jesus Christ from the dead,

To an inheritance incorruptible, and undefiled, and that fadeth not away, reserved in heaven for you,

Who are kept by the power of God through faith unto salvation ready to be revealed in the last time.

Wherein ye greatly rejoice, though now for a season, if need be, ye are in heaviness through manifold temptations:

That the trial of your faith, being much more precious than of gold that perisheth, though it be tried with fire, might be found unto praise and honour and glory at the appearing of Jesus Christ:

Whom having not seen, ye love; in whom, though now ye see him not, yet believing, ye rejoice with joy unspeakable and full of glory:

Receiving the end of your faith, even the salvation of your souls.

I Peter 1:3-9

I have fought a good fight, I have finished my course, I have kept the faith:

Henceforth there is laid up for me a crown of righteousness, which the Lord, the righteous judge, shall give me at that day: and not to me only, but unto all them also that love his appearing.

II Timothy 4:7, 8

The wisdom you seek for your children

My son, attend unto my wisdom, and bow thine ear to my understanding:

That thou mayest regard discretion, and that thy lips may keep knowledge.

Proverbs 5:1, 2

The fear of the Lord is the beginning of wisdom: a good understanding have all they that do his commandments: his praise endureth for ever.

Psalms 111:10

The days of our years are threescore years and ten; and if by reason of strength they be fourscore years, yet is their strength labour and sorrow; for it is soon cut off, and we fly away.

Who knoweth the power of thine anger? even according to thy fear, so is thy wrath.

So teach us to number our days, that we may apply our hearts unto wisdom.

Psalms 90:10-12

O how love I thy law! it is my meditation all the day.

Thou through thy commandments hast made me wiser than mine enemies: for they are ever with me.

I have more understanding than all my teachers: for thy testimonies are my meditation.

I understand more than the ancients, because I keep thy precepts.

I have refrained my feet from every evil way, that I might keep thy word.

I have not departed from thy judgments: for thou hast taught me.

How sweet are thy words unto my taste! yea, sweeter than honey to my mouth!

Through thy precepts I get understanding: therefore I hate every false way.

Psalms 119:97-104

Get wisdom, get understanding: forget it not; neither decline from the words of my mouth.

Forsake her not, and she shall preserve thee: love her, and she shall keep thee.

Wisdom is the principal thing; therefore get wisdom: and with all thy getting get understanding.

Exalt her, and she shall promote thee: she shall bring thee to honour, when thou dost embrace her.

She shall give to thine head an ornament of grace: a crown of glory shall she deliver to thee.

Hear, O my son, and receive my sayings; and the years of thy life shall be many.

I have taught thee in the way of wisdom; I have led thee in right paths.

Proverbs 4:5-11

How much better is it to get wisdom than gold! and to get understanding rather to be chosen than silver!

Proverbs 16:16

Happy is the man that findeth wisdom, and the man that getteth understanding.

For the merchandise of it is better than the merchandise of silver, and the gain thereof than fine gold.

She is more precious than rubies; and all the things thou canst desire are not to be compared unto her.

Length of days is in her right hand; and in her left hand riches and honour.

Her ways are ways of pleasantness, and all her paths are peace.

She is a tree of life to them that lay hold upon her; and happy is every one that retaineth her.

The Lord by wisdom hath founded the earth; by understanding hath he established the heavens.

By his knowledge the depths are broken up, and the clouds drop down the dew.

My son, let not them depart from thine eyes: keep sound wisdom and discretion:

So shall they be life unto thy soul, and grace to thy neck.

Proverbs 3:13-22

Howbeit we speak wisdom among them that are perfect: yet not the wisdom of this world, nor of the princes of this world, that come to nought:

But we speak the wisdom of God in a mystery, even the hidden wisdom, which God ordained before the world unto our glory:

Which none of the princes of this world knew: for had they known it, they would not have crucified the Lord of glory.

But as it is written, Eye hath not seen, nor ear heard, neither have entered into the heart of man, the things which God hath prepared for them that love him.

I Corinthians 2:6-9

But the wisdom that is from above is first pure, then peaceable, gentle, and easy to be intreated, full of mercy and good fruits, without partiality, and without hypocrisy.

James 3:17

If any of you lack wisdom, let him ask of God, that giveth to all men liberally, and upbraideth not; and it shall be given him.

But let him ask in faith, nothing wavering. For he that wavereth is like a wave of the sea driven with the wind and tossed.

James 1:5, 6

His peace in troubled times

The Lord doth build up Jerusalem: he gathereth together the outcasts of Israel.

He healeth the broken in heart, and bindeth up their wounds.

Great is our Lord, and of great power: his understanding is infinite.

The Lord lifteth up the meek: he casteth the wicked down to the ground.

For he hath strengthened the bars of thy gates; he hath blessed thy children within thee.

He maketh peace in thy borders, and filleth thee with the finest of the wheat.

Psalms 147: 2,3,5,6,13,14

An horse is a vain thing for safety: neither shall he deliver any by his great strength.

Behold, the eye of the Lord is upon them that fear him, upon them that hope in his mercy;

To deliver their soul from death, and to keep them alive in famine.

Our soul waiteth for the Lord: he is our help and our shield.

For our heart shall rejoice in him, because we have trusted in his holy name.

Let thy mercy, O Lord, be upon us, according as we hope in thee.

Psalms: 33:17-22

Peace I leave with you, my peace I give unto you: not as the world giveth, give I unto you. Let not your heart be troubled, neither let it be afraid.

John 14:27

Casting all your care upon him; for he careth for you.

Be sober, be vigilant; because your adversary the devil, as a roaring lion, walketh about, seeking whom he may devour:

Whom resist stedfast in the faith, knowing that the same afflictions are accomplished in your brethren that are in the world.

But the God of all grace, who hath called us unto his eternal glory by Christ Jesus, after that ye have suffered a while, make you perfect, stablish, strengthen, settle you.

To him be glory and dominion for ever and ever. Amen.

I Peter 5: 7-11

Ye are of God, little children, and have overcome them: because greater is he that is in you, than he that is in the world.

I John 4:4

I will bless the Lord at all times: his praise shall continually be in my mouth.

My soul shall make her boast in the Lord; the humble shall hear thereof, and be glad.

O magnify the Lord with me, and let us exalt his name together.

I sought the Lord, and he heard me, and delivered me from all my fears.

They looked unto him, and were lightened: and their faces were not ashamed.

This poor man cried, and the Lord heard him, and saved him out of all his troubles.

The angel of the Lord encampeth round about them that fear him, and delivereth them.

O taste and see that the Lord is good: blessed is the man that trusteth in him.

Psalms 34:1-8

Turn thee unto me, and have mercy upon me; for I am desolate and afflicted.

The troubles of my heart are enlarged: O bring thou me out of my distresses.

Look upon mine affliction and my pain; and forgive all my sins.

Psalms 25:16-18

I will be glad and rejoice in thy mercy: for thou hast considered my trouble; thou hast known my soul in adversities;

Psalms 31:7

Victory over the sins in your life

Therefore if any man be in Christ, he is a new creature: old things are passed away; behold, all things are become new.

And all things are of God, who hath reconciled us to himself by Jesus Christ, and hath given to us the ministry of reconciliation;

To wit, that God was in Christ, reconciling the world unto himself, not imputing their trespasses unto them; and hath committed unto us the word of reconciliation.

Now then we are ambassadors for Christ, as though God did beseech you by us: we pray you in Christ's stead, be ye reconciled to God.

For he hath made him to be sin for us, who knew no sin; that we might be made the righteousness of God in him.

II Corinthians 5:17-21

O God, thou knowest my foolishness; and my sins are not hid from thee.

Psalms 69:5

Wash you, make you clean; put away the evil of your doings from before mine eyes; cease to do evil;

Learn to do well; seek judgment, relieve the oppressed, judge the fatherless, plead for the widow.

Come now, and let us reason together, saith the Lord: though your sins be as scarlet, they shall be as white as snow; though they be red like crimson, they shall be as wool.

If ye be willing and obedient, ye shall eat the good of the land:

Isaiah 1:16-19

Therefore seeing we have this ministry, as we have received mercy, we faint not;

But have renounced the hidden things of dishonesty, not walking in craftiness, nor handling the word of God deceitfully; but by manifestation of the truth commending ourselves to every man's conscience in the sight of God.

But if our gospel be hid, it is hid to them that are lost:

In whom the god of this world hath blinded the minds of them which believe not, lest the light of the glorious gospel of Christ, who is the image of God, should shine unto them.

For we preach not ourselves, but Christ Jesus the Lord; and ourselves your servants for Jesus' sake.

For God, who commanded the light to shine out of darkness, hath shined in our hearts, to give the light of the knowledge of the glory of God in the face of Jesus Christ.

II Corinthians 4:1-6

For as many as are of the works of the law are under the curse: for it is written, Cursed is every one that continueth not in all things which are written in the book of the law to do them.

But that no man is justified by the law in the sight of God, it is evident: for, The just shall live by faith.

Galatians 3:10, 11

This then is the message which we have heard of him, and declare unto you, that God is light, and in him is no darkness at all.

If we say that we have fellowship with him, and walk in darkness, we lie, and do not the truth:

But if we walk in the light, as he is in the light, we have fellowship one with another, and the blood of Jesus Christ his Son cleanseth us from all sin.

If we say that we have no sin, we deceive ourselves, and the truth is not in us.

If we confess our sins, he is faithful and just to forgive us our sins, and to cleanse us from all unrighteousness.

If we say that we have not sinned, we make him a liar, and his word is not in us.

I John 1:5-10

Stand fast therefore in the liberty wherewith Christ hath made us free, and be not entangled again with the yoke of bondage.

Galatians 5:1

O death, where is thy sting? O grave, where is thy victory?

The sting of death is sin; and the strength of sin is the law.

But thanks be to God, which giveth us the victory through our Lord Jesus Christ.

Therefore, my beloved brethren, be ye stedfast, unmoveable, always abounding in the work of the Lord, forasmuch as ye know that your labour is not in vain in the Lord.

I Corinthians 15:55-58

Finally, my brethren, be strong in the Lord, and in the power of his might.

Put on the whole armour of God, that ye may be able to stand against the wiles of the devil.

For we wrestle not against flesh and blood, but against principalities, against powers, against the rulers of the darkness of this world, against spiritual wickedness in high places.

Wherefore take unto you the whole armour of God, that ye may be able to withstand in the evil day, and having done all, to stand.

Stand therefore, having your loins girt about with truth, and having on the breastplate of righteousness;

And your feet shod with the preparation of the gospel of peace;

Above all, taking the shield of faith, wherewith ye shall be able to quench all the fiery darts of the wicked.

And take the helmet of salvation, and the sword of the Spirit, which is the word of God:

Praying always with all prayer, and supplication in the Spirit, and watching thereunto with all perseverance and supplication for all saints;

Ephesians 6:10-18

Power to defeat your deepest fears

And God heard the voice of the lad; and the angel of God called to Hagar out of heaven, and said unto her, What aileth thee, Hagar? fear not; for God hath heard the voice of the lad where he is.

Arise, lift up the lad, and hold him in thine hand; for I will make him a great nation.

And God opened her eyes, and she saw a well of water; and she went, and filled the bottle with water, and gave the lad drink.

And God was with the lad; and he grew, and dwelt in the wilderness, and became an archer.

Genesis 21:17-20

O magnify the Lord with me, and let us exalt his name together.

I sought the Lord, and he heard me, and delivered me from all my fears.

They looked unto him, and were lightened: and their faces were not ashamed.

This poor man cried, and the Lord heard him, and saved him out of all his troubles.

The angel of the Lord encampeth round about them that fear him, and delivereth them.

O taste and see that the Lord is good: blessed is the man that trusteth in him.

Psalms 34:3-8

And Joshua the son of Nun, and Caleb the son of Jephunneh, which were of them that searched the land, rent their clothes:

And they spake unto all the company of the children of Israel, saying, The land, which we passed through to search it, is an exceeding good land.

If the Lord delight in us, then he will bring us into this land, and give it us; a land which floweth with milk and honey.

Only rebel not ye against the Lord, neither fear ye the people of the land; for they are bread for us: their defence is departed from them, and the Lord is with us: fear them not.

Numbers 14:6-9

Be not afraid of sudden fear, neither of the desolation of the wicked, when it cometh.

For the Lord shall be thy confidence, and shall keep thy foot from being taken.

Proverbs 3:25, 26

Behold, the Lord thy God hath set the land before thee: go up and possess it, as the Lord God of thy fathers hath said unto thee; fear not, neither be discouraged.

And ye came near unto me every one of you, and said, We will send men before us, and they shall search us out the land, and bring us word again by what way we must go up, and into what cities we shall come.

And the saying pleased me well: and I took twelve men of you, one of a tribe:

And they turned and went up into the mountain, and came unto the valley of Eshcol, and searched it out.

And they took of the fruit of the land in their hands, and brought it down unto us, and brought us word again, and said, It is a good land which the Lord our God doth give us.

Notwithstanding ye would not go up, but rebelled against the commandment of the Lord your God:

And ye murmured in your tents, and said, Because the Lord hated us, he hath brought us forth out of the land of Egypt, to deliver us into the hand of the Amorites, to destroy us.

Whither shall we go up? our brethren have discouraged our heart, saying, The people is greater and taller than we; the cities are great and walled up to heaven; and moreover we have seen the sons of the Anakims there.

Then I said unto you, Dread not, neither be afraid of them.

The Lord your God which goeth before you, he shall fight for you, according to all that he did for you in Egypt before your eyes;

And in the wilderness, where thou hast seen how that the Lord thy God bare thee, as a man doth bear his son, in all the way that ye went, until ye came into this place.

Deuteronomy 1:21-31

After these things the word of the Lord came unto Abram in a vision, saying, Fear not, Abram: I am thy shield, and thy exceeding great reward.

Genesis 15:1

Wherefore should I fear in the days of evil, when the iniquity of my heels shall compass me about?

They that trust in their wealth, and boast themselves in the multitude of their riches;

But God will redeem my soul from the power of the grave: for he shall receive me. Selah.

Be not thou afraid when one is made rich, when the glory of his house is increased;

For when he dieth he shall carry nothing away: his glory shall not descend after him.

Psalms 49:5, 6, 15-17

Nay, in all these things we are more than conquerors through him that loved us.

For I am persuaded, that neither death, nor life, nor angels, nor principalities, nor powers, or things present, nor things to come,

Nor height, nor depth, nor any other creature, shall be able to separate us from the love of God, which is in Christ Jesus our Lord.

Romans 8:37-39

The courage to be a man of integrity

Blessed is the man that walketh not in the counsel of the ungodly, nor standeth in the way of sinners, nor sitteth in the seat of the scornful.

But his delight is in the law of the Lord; and in his law doth he meditate day and night.

And he shall be like a tree planted by the rivers of water, that bringeth forth his fruit in his season; his leaf also shall not wither; and whatsoever he doeth shall prosper.

The ungodly are not so: but are like the chaff which the wind driveth away.

Therefore the ungodly shall not stand in the judgment, nor sinners in the congregation of the righteous.

For the Lord knoweth the way of the righteous: but the way of the ungodly shall perish.

Psalms 1:1-6

A good man sheweth favour, and lendeth: he will guide his affairs with discretion.

Surely he shall not be moved for ever: the righteous shall be in everlasting remembrance.

He shall not be afraid of evil tidings: his heart is fixed, trusting in the Lord.

Psalms 112:5-7

Blessed are the undefiled in the way, who walk in the law of the Lord.

Blessed are they that keep his testimonies, and that seek him with the whole heart.

They also do no iniquity: they walk in his ways.

Thou hast commanded us to keep thy precepts diligently.

O that my ways were directed to keep thy statutes!

Then shall I not be ashamed, when I have respect unto all thy commandments.

I will praise thee with uprightness of heart, when I shall have learned thy righteous judgments.

I will keep thy statutes: O forsake me not utterly.

Psalms 119:1-8

Then stood up Phinehas, and executed judgment: and so the plague was stayed.

And that was counted unto him for righteousness unto all generations for evermore.

Psalms 106:30, 31

A false balance is abomination to the Lord: but a just weight is his delight.

When pride cometh, then cometh shame: but with the lowly is wisdom.

The integrity of the upright shall guide them: but the perverseness of transgressors shall destroy them.

Proverbs 11:1-3

Divers weights are an abomination unto the Lord; and a false balance is not good.

Proverbs 20:23

He that speaketh truth sheweth forth righteousness: but a false witness deceit.

There is that speaketh like the piercings of a sword: but the tongue of the wise is health.

The lip of truth shall be established for ever: but a lying tongue is but for a moment.

Proverbs 12:17-19

The Lord shall judge the people: judge me, O Lord, according to my righteousness, and according to mine integrity that is in me.

Psalms 7:8

I will behave myself wisely in a perfect way. O when wilt thou come unto me? I will walk within my house with a perfect heart.

I will set no wicked thing before mine eyes: I hate the work of them that turn aside; it shall not cleave to me.

A froward heart shall depart from me: I will not know a wicked person.

Whoso privily slandereth his neighbour, him will I cut off: him that hath an high look and a proud heart will not I suffer.

Mine eyes shall be upon the faithful of the land, that they may dwell with me: he that walketh in a perfect way, he shall serve me.

He that worketh deceit shall not dwell within my house: he that telleth lies shall not tarry in my sight.

I will early destroy all the wicked of the land; that I may cut off all wicked doers from the city of the Lord.

Psalms 101:2-8

God Asks You To...

Instruct your children in His Word

Hear, ye children, the instruction of a father, and attend to know understanding.

For I give you good doctrine, forsake ye not my law.

For I was my father's son, tender and only beloved in the sight of my mother.

He taught me also, and said unto me, Let thine heart retain my words: keep my commandments, and live.

Proverbs 4:1-4

Give ear, O my people, to my law: incline your ears to the words of my mouth.

I will open my mouth in a parable: I will utter dark sayings of old:

Which we have heard and known, and our fathers have told us.

We will not hide them from their children, shewing to the generation to come the praises of the Lord, and his strength, and his wonderful works that he hath done.

For he established a testimony in Jacob, and appointed a law in Israel, which he commanded our fathers, that they should make them known to their children:

That the generation to come might know them, even the children which should be born; who should arise and declare them to their children:

That they might set their hope in God, and not forget the works of God, but keep his commandments:

And might not be as their fathers, a stubborn and rebellious generation; a generation that set not their heart aright, and whose spirit was not stedfast with God.

Psalms 78:1-8

A wise man will hear, and will increase learning; and a man of understanding shall attain unto wise counsels:

To understand a proverb, and the interpretation; the words of the wise, and their dark sayings.

The fear of the Lord is the beginning of knowledge: but fools despise wisdom and instruction.

My son, hear the instruction of thy father, and forsake not the law of thy mother:

For they shall be an ornament of grace unto thy head, and chains about thy neck.

Proverbs 1:5-9

I write not these things to shame you, but as my beloved sons I warn you.

For though ye have ten thousand instructors in Christ, yet have ye not many fathers: for in Christ Jesus I have begotten you through the gospel.

Wherefore I beseech you, be ye followers of me.

For this cause have I sent unto you Timotheus, who is my beloved son, and faithful in the Lord, who shall bring you into remembrance of my ways which be in Christ, as I teach every where in every church.

Now some are puffed up, as though I would not come to you.

But I will come to you shortly, if the Lord will, and will know, not the speech of them which are puffed up, but the power.

For the kingdom of God is not in word, but in power.

What will ye? shall I come unto you with a rod, or in love, and in the spirit of meekness?

I Corinthians 4:14-21

Now therefore hearken unto me, O ye children: for blessed are they that keep my ways.

Hear instruction, and be wise, and refuse it not.

Blessed is the man that heareth me, watching daily at my gates, waiting at the posts of my doors.

For whoso findeth me findeth life, and shall obtain favour of the Lord.

Proverbs 8:32-35

All scripture is given by inspiration of God, and is profitable for doctrine, for reproof, for correction, for instruction in righteousness:

II Timothy 3:16

For the word of God is quick, and powerful, and sharper than any twoedged sword, piercing even to the dividing asunder of soul and spirit, and of the joints and marrow, and is a discerner of the thoughts and intents of the heart.

Hebrews 4:12

But be ye doers of the word, and not hearers only, deceiving your own selves.

James 1:22

My son, attend to my words; incline thine ear unto my sayings.

Let them not depart from thine eyes; keep them in the midst of thine heart.

For they are life unto those that find them, and health to all their flesh.

Proverbs 4:20-22

Wherefore laying aside all malice, and all guile, and hypocrisies, and envies, and all evil speakings,

As newborn babes, desire the sincere milk of the word, that ye may grow thereby:

I Peter 2:1, 2

For all flesh is as grass, and all the glory of man as the flower of grass. The grass withereth, and the flower thereof falleth away:

But the word of the Lord endureth for ever. And this is the word which by the gospel is preached unto you.

I Peter 1:24, 25

I will go in the strength of the Lord God: I will make mention of thy righteousness, even of thine only.

O God, thou hast taught me from my youth: and hitherto have I declared thy wondrous works.

Now also when I am old and grayheaded, O God, forsake me not; until I have shewed thy strength unto this generation, and thy power to every one that is to come.

Psalms 71:16-18

Teach your children to pray

But will God indeed dwell on the earth? behold, the heaven and heaven of heavens cannot contain thee; how much less this house that I have builded?

Yet have thou respect unto the prayer of thy servant, and to his supplication, O Lord my God, to hearken unto the cry and to the prayer, which thy servant prayeth before thee to day:

That thine eyes may be open toward this house night and day, even toward the place of which thou hast said, My name shall be there: that thou mayest hearken unto the prayer which thy servant shall make toward this place.

And hearken thou to the supplication of thy servant, and of thy people Israel, when they shall pray toward this place: and hear thou in heaven thy dwelling place: and when thou hearest, forgive.

I Kings 8:27-30

Let us therefore come boldly unto the throne of grace, that we may obtain mercy, and find grace to help in time of need.

Hebrews 4:16

For thou, O Lord of hosts, God of Israel, hast revealed to thy servant, saying, I will build thee an house: therefore hath thy servant found in his heart to pray this prayer unto thee.

And now, O Lord God, thou art that God, and thy words be true, and thou hast promised this goodness unto thy servant:

II Samuel 7:27, 28

Therefore I say unto you, What things soever ye desire, when ye pray, believe that ye receive them, and ye shall have them.

Mark 11:24

Call unto me, and I will answer thee, and shew thee great and mighty things, which thou knowest not.

Jeremiah 33:3

For we are saved by hope: but hope that is seen is not hope: for what a man seeth, why doth he yet hope for?

But if we hope for that we see not, then do we with patience wait for it.

Likewise the Spirit also helpeth our infirmities: for we know not what we should pray for as we ought: but the Spirit itself maketh intercession for us with groanings which cannot be uttered.

And he that searcheth the hearts knoweth what is the mind of the Spirit, because he maketh intercession for the saints according to the will of God.

And we know that all things work together for good to them that love God, to them who are the called according to his purpose.

Romans 8:24-28

And whatsoever we ask, we receive of him, because we keep his commandments, and do those things that are pleasing in his sight.

I John 3:22

And when thou prayest, thou shalt not be as the hypocrites are: for they love to pray standing in the synagogues and in the corners of the streets, that they may be seen of men. Verily I say unto you, They have their reward.

But thou, when thou prayest, enter into thy closet, and when thou hast shut thy door, pray to thy Father which is in secret; and thy Father which seeth in secret shall reward thee openly.

But when ye pray, use not vain repetitions, as the heathen do: for they think that they shall be heard for their much speaking.

Be not ye therefore like unto them: for your Father knoweth what things ye have need of, before ye ask him.

After this manner therefore pray ye: Our Father which art in heaven, Hallowed be thy name.

Thy kingdom come. Thy will be done in earth, as it is in heaven.

Give us this day our daily bread.

And forgive us our debts, as we forgive our debtors.

And lead us not into temptation, but deliver us from evil: For thine is the kingdom, and the power, and the glory, for ever. Amen.

Matthew 6:5-13

And it shall come to pass, that before they call, I will answer; and while they are yet speaking, I will hear.

Isaiah 65:24

These things have I written unto you that believe on the name of the Son of God; that ye may know that ye have eternal life, and that ye may believe on the name of the Son of God.

And this is the confidence that we have in him, that, if we ask any thing according to his will, he heareth us:

And if we know that he hear us, whatsoever we ask, we know that we have the petitions that we desired of him.

I John 5:13-15

Reach out to families who are homeless

And thou shalt rejoice before the Lord thy God, thou, and thy son, and thy daughter, and thy manservant, and thy maidservant, and the Levite that is within thy gates, and the stranger, and the fatherless, and the widow, that are among you, in the place which the Lord thy God hath chosen to place his name there.

Deuteronomy 16:11

Whoso stoppeth his ears at the cry of the poor, he also shall cry himself, but shall not be heard.

Proverbs 21:13

Yet they seek me daily, and delight to know my ways, as a nation that did righteousness, and forsook not the ordinance of their God: they ask of me the ordinances of justice; they take delight in approaching to God.

Isaiah 58:2

Is it not to deal thy bread to the hungry, and that thou bring the poor that are cast out to thy house? when thou seest the naked, that thou cover him; and that thou hide not thyself from thine own flesh?

Then shall thy light break forth as the morning, and thine health shall spring forth speedily: and thy righteousness shall go before thee: the glory of the Lord shall be thy reward.

Then shalt thou call, and the Lord shall answer; thou shalt cry, and he shall say, Here I am. If thou take away from the midst of thee the yoke, the putting forth of the finger, and speaking vanity;

And if thou draw out thy soul to the hungry, and satisfy the afflicted soul; then shall thy light rise in obscurity, and thy darkness be as the noon day:

And the Lord shall guide thee continually, and satisfy thy soul in drought, and make fat thy bones: and thou shalt be like a watered garden, and like a spring of water, whose waters fail not.

Isaiah 58:7-11

Then shall the King say unto them on his right hand, Come, ye blessed of my Father, inherit the kingdom prepared for you from the foundation of the world:

For I was an hungered, and ye gave me meat: I was thirsty, and ye gave me drink: I was a stranger, and ye took me in:

Naked, and ye clothed me: I was sick, and ye visited me: I was in prison, and ye came unto me.

Then shall the righteous answer him, saying, Lord, when saw we thee an hungered, and fed thee? or thirsty, and gave thee drink?

When saw we thee a stranger, and took thee in? or naked, and clothed thee?

Or when saw we thee sick, or in prison, and came unto thee?

And the King shall answer and say unto them, Verily I say unto you, Inasmuch as ye have done it unto one of the least of these my brethren, ye have done it unto me.

Matthew 25:34-40

Happy is he that hath the God of Jacob for his help, whose hope is in the Lord his God:

Which made heaven, and earth, the sea, and all that therein is: which keepeth truth for ever:

Which executeth judgment for the oppressed: which giveth food to the hungry. The Lord looseth the prisoners:

The Lord openeth the eyes of the blind: the Lord raiseth them that are bowed down: the Lord loveth the righteous:

The Lord preserveth the strangers; he relieveth the fatherless and widow: but the way of the wicked he turneth upside down.

The Lord shall reign for ever, even thy God, O Zion, unto all generations. Praise ye the Lord.

Psalms 146:5-10

Let brotherly love continue.

Be not forgetful to entertain strangers: for thereby some have entertained angels unawares.

Hebrews 13:1, 2

And above all things have fervent charity among yourselves: for charity shall cover the multitude of sins.

Use hospitality one to another without grudging.

As every man hath received the gift, even so minister the same one to another, as good stewards of the manifold grace of God.

I Peter 4:8-10

But whoso hath this world's good, and seeth his brother have need, and shutteth up his bowels of compassion from him, how dwelleth the love of God in him?

My little children, let us not love in word, neither in tongue; but in deed and in truth.

And hereby we know that we are of the truth, and shall assure our hearts before him.

I John 3:17-19

And when ye reap the harvest of your land, thou shalt not wholly reap the corners of thy field, neither shalt thou gather the gleanings of thy harvest.

And thou shalt not glean thy vineyard, neither shalt thou gather every grape of thy vineyard; thou shalt leave them for the poor and stranger: I am the Lord your God.

Leviticus 19:9, 10

Love your neighbors

Thou shalt love thy neighbour as thyself.
Matthew 19:19b

Say not unto thy neighbour, Go, and come again, and tomorrow I will give; when thou hast it by thee.
Devise not evil against thy neighbour, seeing he dwelleth securely by thee.
Proverbs 3:28, 29

He that despiseth his neighbour sinneth: but he that hath mercy on the poor, happy is he.
Proverbs 14:21

He that is void of wisdom despiseth his neighbour: but a man of understanding holdeth his peace.
Proverbs 11:12

Thou shalt not defraud thy neighbour, neither rob him:
Leviticus 19:13a

Go not forth hastily to strive, lest thou know not what to do in the end thereof, when thy neighbour hath put thee to shame.
Debate thy cause with thy neighbour himself: and discover not a secret to another:
Proverbs 25:8, 9

Thou shalt not bear false witness against thy neighbour.

Thou shalt not covet thy neighbour's house, thou shalt not covet thy neighbour's wife, nor his manservant, nor his maidservant, nor his ox, nor his ass, nor any thing that is thy neighbour's.

Exodus 20:16, 17

Whoso privily slandereth his neighbour, him will I cut off: him that hath an high look and a proud heart will not I suffer.

Mine eyes shall be upon the faithful of the land, that they may dwell with me: he that walketh in a perfect way, he shall serve me.

He that worketh deceit shall not dwell within my house: he that telleth lies shall not tarry in my sight.

Psalms 101:5-7

And be not conformed to this world: but be ye transformed by the renewing of your mind, that ye may prove what is that good, and acceptable, and perfect, will of God.

For I say, through the grace given unto me, to every man that is among you, not to think of himself more highly than he ought to think; but to think soberly, according as God hath dealt to every man the measure of faith.

Romans 12:2, 3

But he, willing to justify himself, said unto Jesus, And who is my neighbour?

And Jesus answering said, A certain man went down from Jerusalem to Jericho, and fell among thieves, which stripped him of his raiment, and wounded him, and departed, leaving him half dead.

And by chance there came down a certain priest that way: and when he saw him, he passed by on the other side.

And likewise a Levite, when he was at the place, came and looked on him, and passed by on the other side.

But a certain Samaritan, as he journeyed, came where he was: and when he saw him, he had compassion on him,

And went to him, and bound up his wounds, pouring in oil and wine, and set him on his own beast, and brought him to an inn, and took care of him.

And on the morrow when he departed, he took out two pence, and gave them to the host, and said unto him, Take care of him; and whatsoever thou spendest more, when I come again, I will repay thee.

Which now of these three, thinkest thou, was neighbour unto him that fell among the thieves?

And he said, He that shewed mercy on him. Then said Jesus unto him, Go, and do thou likewise.

Luke 10:29-37

Teach your children gratitude

If so be ye have tasted that the Lord is gracious.

I Peter 2:3

Make a joyful noise unto the Lord, all ye lands.

Serve the Lord with gladness come before his presence with singing.

Psalms 100:1, 2

And that their children, which have not known any thing, may hear, and learn to fear the Lord your God, as long as ye live in the land whither ye go over Jordan to possess it.

Deuteronomy 31:13

Now therefore write ye this song for you, and teach it the children of Israel: put it in their mouths, that this song may be a witness for me against the children of Israel.

For when I shall have brought them into the land which I sware unto their fathers, that floweth with milk and honey; and they shall have eaten and filled themselves, and waxen fat; then will they turn unto other gods, and serve them, and provoke me, and break my covenant.

And it shall come to pass, when many evils and troubles are befallen them, that this song shall testify against them as a witness; for it shall not be forgotten out of the mouths of their seed: for I know their imagination which they go about, even now, before I have brought them into the land which I sware.

Deuteronomy 31:19-21

Let your conversation be without covetousness; and be content with such things as ye have: for he hath said, I will never leave thee, nor forsake thee.

Hebrews 13:5

And my spirit hath rejoiced in God my Saviour.

Luke 1:47

Finally, brethren, whatsoever things are true, whatsoever things are honest, whatsoever things are just, whatsoever things are pure, whatsoever things are lovely, whatsoever things are of good report; if there be any virtue, and if there be any praise, think on these things.

Those things, which ye have both learned, and received, and heard, and seen in me, do: and the God of peace shall be with you.

But I rejoiced in the Lord greatly, that now at the last your care of me hath flourished again; wherein ye were also careful, but ye lacked opportunity.

Not that I speak in respect of want: for I have learned, in whatsoever state I am, therewith to be content.

Philippians 4:8-11

Sing unto the Lord, O ye saints of his, and give thanks at the remembrance of his holiness.

For his anger endureth but a moment; in his favour is life: weeping may endure for a night, but joy cometh in the morning.

And in my prosperity I said, I shall never be moved.

Psalms 30:4-6

And it came to pass, as he went to Jerusalem, that he passed through the midst of Samaria and Galilee.

And as he entered into a certain village, there met him ten men that were lepers, which stood afar off:

And they lifted up their voices, and said, Jesus, Master, have mercy on us.

And when he saw them, he said unto them, Go shew yourselves unto the priests. And it came to pass, that, as they went, they were cleansed.

And one of them, when he saw that he was healed, turned back, and with a loud voice glorified God,

And fell down on his face at his feet, giving him thanks: and he was a Samaritan.

And Jesus answering said, Were there not ten cleansed? but where are the nine?

There are not found that returned to give glory to God, save this stranger.

And he said unto him, Arise, go thy way: thy faith hath made thee whole.

Luke 17:11-19

But I determined this with myself, that I would not come again to you in heaviness.

For if I make you sorry, who is he then that maketh me glad, but the same which is made sorry by me?

And I wrote this same unto you, lest, when I came, I should have sorrow from them of whom I ought to rejoice; having confidence in you all, that my joy is the joy of you all.

II Corinthians 2:1-3

Show kindness to your family

Or what man is there of you, whom if his son ask bread, will he give him a stone?

Or if he ask a fish, will he give him a serpent?

If ye then, being evil, know how to give good gifts unto your children, how much more shall your Father which is in heaven give good things to them that ask him?

Matthew 7:9-11

And his father Isaac said unto him, Come near now, and kiss me, my son.

Genesis 27:26

I lead in the way of righteousness, in the midst of the paths of judgment:

That I may cause those that love me to inherit substance; and I will fill their treasures.

The Lord possessed me in the beginning of his way, before his works of old.

Proverbs 8:20-22

Now therefore, I pray you, swear unto me by the Lord, since I have shewed you kindness, that ye will also shew kindness unto my father's house, and give me a true token:

And that ye will save alive my father, and my mother, and my brethren, and my sisters, and all that they have, and deliver our lives from death.

And the men answered her, Our life for yours, if ye utter not this our business. And it shall be, when the Lord hath given us the land, that we will deal kindly and truly with thee.

Joshua 2:12-14

He that hath no rule over his own spirit is like a city that is broken down, and without walls.

Proverbs 25:28

But so shall it not be among you: but whosoever will be great among you, shall be your minister:

And whosoever of you will be the chiefest, shall be servant of all.

For even the Son of man came not to be ministered unto, but to minister, and to give his life a ransom for many.

Mark 10:43-45

Be not overcome of evil, but overcome evil with good.

Romans 12:21

Let all bitterness, and wrath, and anger, and clamour, and evil speaking, be put away from you, with all malice:

And be ye kind one to another, tenderhearted, forgiving one another, even as God for Christ's sake hath forgiven you.

Ephesians 4:31, 32

And Naomi said unto her two daughters in law, Go, return each to her mother's house: the Lord deal kindly with you, as ye have dealt with the dead, and with me.

Ruth 1:8

Hatred stirreth up strifes: but love covereth all sins.

Proverbs 10:12

We then that are strong ought to bear the infirmities of the weak, and not to please ourselves.

Romans 15:1

And Joseph said unto them, Fear not: for am I in the place of God?

But as for you, ye thought evil against me; but God meant it unto good, to bring to pass, as it is this day, to save much people alive.

Now therefore fear ye not: I will nourish you, and your little ones. And he comforted them, and spake kindly unto them.

Genesis 50:19-21

Ye are witnesses, and God also, how holily and justly and unblameably we behaved ourselves among you that believe:

As ye know how we exhorted and comforted and charged every one of you, as a father doth his children,

That ye would walk worthy of God, who hath called you unto his kingdom and glory.

I Thessalonians 2:10-12

Trust Him even when you don't understand.

Behold, he that keepeth Israel shall neither slumber nor sleep.

The Lord is thy keeper: the Lord is thy shade upon thy right hand.

The sun shall not smite thee by day, nor the moon by night.

The Lord shall preserve thee from all evil: he shall preserve thy soul.

The Lord shall preserve thy going out and thy coming in from this time forth, and even for evermore.

Psalms 121:4-8

Some trust in chariots, and some in horses: but we will remember the name of the Lord our God.

They are brought down and fallen: but we are risen, and stand upright.

Save, Lord: let the king hear us when we call.

Psalms 20:7-9

And now men see not the bright light which is in the clouds: but the wind passeth, and cleanseth them.

Fair weather cometh out of the north: with God is terrible majesty.

Touching the Almighty, we cannot find him out: he is excellent in power, and in judgment, and in plenty of justice: he will not afflict.

Men do therefore fear him: he respecteth not any that are wise of heart.

Then the Lord answered Job out of the whirlwind . . . ,

Job 37:21-24, 38:1a

O the depth of the riches both of the wisdom and knowledge of God! how unsearchable are his judgments, and his ways past finding out!

For who hath known the mind of the Lord? or who hath been his counsellor?

Or who hath first given to him, and it shall be recompensed unto him again?

For of him, and through him, and to him, are all things: to whom be glory for ever. Amen.

Romans 11:33-36

Then Job answered and said,

Even to day is my complaint bitter: my stroke is heavier than my groaning.

Oh that I knew where I might find him! that I might come even to his seat!

I would order my cause before him, and fill my mouth with arguments.

I would know the words which he would answer me, and understand what he would say unto me.

Will he plead against me with his great power? No; but he would put strength in me.

There the righteous might dispute with him; so should I be delivered for ever from my judge.

Behold, I go forward, but he is not there; and backward, but I cannot perceive him:

On the left hand, where he doth work, but I cannot behold him: he hideth himself on the right hand, that I cannot see him:

But he knoweth the way that I take: when he hath tried me, I shall come forth as gold.

My foot hath held his steps, his way have I kept, and not declined.

Neither have I gone back from the commandment of his lips; I have esteemed the words of his mouth more than my necessary food.

Job 23:1-12

In the day of my trouble I will call upon thee: for thou wilt answer me.

Among the gods there is none like unto thee, O Lord; neither are there any works like unto thy works.

All nations whom thou hast made shall come and worship before thee, O Lord; and shall glorify thy name.

For thou art great, and doest wondrous things: thou art God alone.

Psalms 86:7-10

Then they cry unto the Lord in their trouble, and he saveth them out of their distresses.

He sent his word, and healed them, and delivered them from their destructions.

Psalms 107:19, 20

Every word of God is pure: he is a shield unto them that put their trust in him.

Proverbs 30:5

Therefore, brethren, we were comforted over you in all our affliction and distress by your faith:

For now we live, if ye stand fast in the Lord.

I Thessalonians 3:7, 8

Speak encouraging words to all

As we have therefore opportunity, let us do good unto all men, especially unto them who are of the household of faith.

Galatians 6:10

Let no corrupt communication proceed out of your mouth, but that which is good to the use of edifying, that it may minister grace unto the hearers.

And grieve not the holy Spirit of God, whereby ye are sealed unto the day of redemption.

Let all bitterness, and wrath, and anger, and clamour, and evil speaking, be put away from you, with all malice:

And be ye kind one to another, tenderhearted, forgiving one another, even as God for Christ's sake hath forgiven you.

Ephesians 4:29-32

Bear ye one another's burdens, and so fulfill the law of Christ.

Galatians 6:2

If any man among you seem to be religious, and bridleth not his tongue, but deceiveth his own heart, this man's religion is vain.

James 1:26

For in many things we offend all. If any man offend not in word, the same is a perfect man, and able also to bridle the whole body.

Behold, we put bits in the horses' mouths, that they may obey us; and we turn about their whole body.

Behold also the ships, which though they be so great, and are driven of fierce winds, yet are they turned about with a very small helm, whithersoever the governor listeth.

Even so the tongue is a little member, and boasteth great things. Behold, how great a matter a little fire kindleth!

And the tongue is a fire, a world of iniquity: so is the tongue among our members, that it defileth the whole body, and setteth on fire the course of nature; and it is set on fire of hell.

For every kind of beasts, and of birds, and of serpents, and of things in the sea, is tamed, and hath been tamed of mankind:

But the tongue can no man tame; it is an unruly evil, full of deadly poison.

Therewith bless we God, even the Father; and therewith curse we men, which are made after the similitude of God.

Out of the same mouth proceedeth blessing and cursing. My brethren, these things ought not so to be.

James 3:2-10

Not rendering evil for evil, or railing for railing: but contrariwise blessing; knowing that ye are thereunto called, that ye should inherit a blessing.

For he that will love life, and see good days, let him refrain his tongue from evil, and his lips that they speak no guile:

I Peter 3:9, 10

There is that speaketh like the piercings of a sword: but the tongue of the wise is health.

Proverbs 12:18

A man hath joy by the answer of his mouth: and a word spoken in due season, how good is it!

Proverbs 15:23

The wilderness and the solitary place shall be glad for them; and the desert shall rejoice, and blossom as the rose.

It shall blossom abundantly, and rejoice even with joy and singing: the glory of Lebanon shall be given unto it, the excellency of Carmel and Sharon, they shall see the glory of the Lord, and the excellency of our God.

Strengthen ye the weak hands, and confirm the feeble knees.

Say to them that are of a fearful heart, Be strong, fear not: behold, your God will come with vengeance, even God with a recompence; he will come and save you.

Isaiah 35:1-4

For out of the abundance of the heart the mouth speaketh.

But I say unto you, That every idle word that men shall speak, they shall give account thereof in the day of judgment.

For by thy words thou shalt be justified, and by thy words thou shalt be condemned.

Matthew 12:34b, 36, 37

We took sweet counsel together, and walked unto the house of God in company.

Psalms 55:14

For none of us liveth to himself, and no man dieth to himself.

For whether we live, we live unto the Lord; and whether we die, we die unto the Lord: whether we live therefore, or die, we are the Lord's.

For to this end Christ both died, and rose, and revived, that he might be Lord both of the dead and living.

But why dost thou judge thy brother? or why dost thou set at nought thy brother? for we shall all stand before the judgment seat of Christ.

For it is written, As I live, saith the Lord, every knee shall bow to me, and every tongue shall confess to God.

So then every one of us shall give account of himself to God.

Let us not therefore judge one another any more: but judge this rather, that no man put a stumbling-block or an occasion to fall in his brother's way.

I know, and am persuaded by the Lord Jesus, that there is nothing unclean of itself: but to him that esteemeth any thing to be unclean, to him it is unclean.

But if thy brother be grieved with thy meat, now walkest thou not charitably. Destroy not him with thy meat, for whom Christ died.

Let not then your good be evil spoken of:

For the kingdom of God is not meat and drink; but righteousness, and peace, and joy in the Holy Ghost.

For he that in these things serveth Christ is acceptable to God, and approved of men.

Let us therefore follow after the things which make for peace, and things wherewith one may edify another.

Romans 14:7-19

God Gives You Strength When...

You comfort your children in their sorrows

But the mercy of the Lord is from everlasting to everlasting upon them that fear him, and his righteousness unto children's children;

Psalms 103:17

He shall feed his flock like a shepherd: he shall gather the lambs with his arm, and carry them in his bosom, and shall gently lead those that are with young.

Isaiah 40:11

Comfort ye, comfort ye my people, saith your God.

The grass withereth, the flower fadeth: but the word of our God shall stand for ever.

Isaiah 40:1, 8

Fear thou not; for I am with thee: be not dismayed; for I am thy God: I will strengthen thee; yea, I will help thee; yea, I will uphold thee with the right hand of my righteousness.

Behold, I will make thee a new sharp threshing instrument having teeth: thou shalt thresh the mountains, and beat them small, and shalt make the hills as chaff.

Thou shalt fan them, and the wind shall carry them away, and the whirlwind shall scatter them: and thou shalt rejoice in the Lord, and shalt glory in the Holy One of Israel.

Isaiah 41:10, 15, 16

Surely he hath borne our griefs, and carried our sorrows: yet we did esteem him stricken, smitten of God, and afflicted.

But he was wounded for our transgressions, he was bruised for our iniquities: the chastisement of our peace was upon him; and with his stripes we are healed.

Isaiah 53:4, 5

When the waves of death compassed me, the floods of ungodly men made me afraid;

The sorrows of hell compassed me about; the snares of death prevented me;

In my distress I called upon the Lord, and cried to my God: and he did hear my voice out of his temple, and my cry did enter into his ears.

II Samuel 22:5-7

The Lord God which gathereth the outcasts of Israel saith, Yet will I gather others to him, beside those that are gathered unto him.

I have seen his ways, and will heal him: I will lead him also, and restore comforts unto him and to his mourners.

Isaiah 56:8

Sing, O heavens; and be joyful, O earth; and break forth into singing, O mountains: for the Lord hath comforted his people, and will have mercy upon his afflicted.

But Zion said, The Lord hath forsaken me, and my Lord hath forgotten me.

Can a woman forget her sucking child, that she should not have compassion on the son of her womb? yea, they may forget, yet will I not forget thee.

Behold, I have graven thee upon the palms of my hands; thy walls are continually before me.

Isaiah 49:13-16

For I have satiated the weary soul, and I have replenished every sorrowful soul.

Jeremiah 31:25

Are not two sparrows sold for a farthing? and one of them shall not fall on the ground without your Father.

But the very hairs of your head are all numbered.

Fear ye not therefore, ye are of more value than many sparrows.

Matthew 10:29-31

Blessed be God, even the Father of our Lord Jesus Christ, the Father of mercies, and the God of all comfort;

Who comforteth us in all our tribulation, that we may be able to comfort them which are in any trouble, by the comfort wherewith we ourselves are comforted of God.

For as the sufferings of Christ abound in us,
so our consolation also aboundeth by Christ.
II Corinthians 1:3-5

You feel defeated and powerless

God is our refuge and strength, a very present help in trouble.

Therefore will not we fear, though the earth be removed, and though the mountains be carried into the midst of the sea;

Though the waters thereof roar and be troubled, though the mountains shake with the swelling thereof.

Psalms 46:1-3

Although affliction cometh not forth of the dust, neither doth trouble spring out of the ground;

Yet man is born unto trouble, as the sparks fly upward.

I would seek unto God, and unto God would I commit my cause:

Which doeth great things and unsearchable; marvellous things without number:

Job 5:6-9

Give ear to my words, O Lord, consider my meditation.

Hearken unto the voice of my cry, my King, and my God: for unto thee will I pray.

My voice shalt thou hear in the morning, O Lord; in the morning will I direct my prayer unto thee, and will look up.

For thou art not a God that hath pleasure in wickedness: neither shall evil dwell with thee.

The foolish shall not stand in thy sight: thou hatest all workers of iniquity.

Thou shalt destroy them that speak leasing: the Lord will abhor the bloody and deceitful man.

But as for me, I will come into thy house in the multitude of thy mercy: and in thy fear will I worship toward thy holy temple.

Lead me, O Lord, in thy righteousness because of mine enemies; make thy way straight before my face.

But let all those that put their trust in thee rejoice: let them ever shout for joy, because thou defendest them: let them also that love thy name be joyful in thee.

For thou, Lord, wilt bless the righteous; with favour wilt thou compass him as with a shield.

Psalms 5:1-8, 11, 12

For this thing I besought the Lord thrice, that it might depart from me.

And he said unto me, My grace is sufficient for thee: for my strength is made perfect in weakness. Most gladly therefore will I rather glory in my infirmities, that the power of Christ may rest upon me.

Therefore I take pleasure in infirmities, in reproaches, in necessities, in persecutions, in distresses for Christ's sake: for when I am weak, then am I strong.

II Corinthians 12:8-10

And they that know thy name will put their trust in thee: for thou, Lord, hast not forsaken them that seek thee.

Psalms 9:10

Thou art my hiding place and my shield: I hope in thy word.

Psalms 119:114

Give us help from trouble: for vain is the help of man.

Through God we shall do valiantly: for he it is that shall tread down our enemies.

Psalms 108:12, 13

He that dwelleth in the secret place of the most High shall abide under the shadow of the Almighty.

I will say of the Lord, He is my refuge and my fortress: my God, in him will I trust.

Surely he shall deliver thee from the snare of the fowler, and from the noisome pestilence.

He shall cover thee with his feathers, and under his wings shalt thou trust: his truth shall be thy shield and buckler.

Thou shalt not be afraid for the terror by night; nor for the arrow that flieth by day;

Nor for the pestilence that walketh in darkness; nor for the destruction that wasteth at noonday.

A thousand shall fall at thy side, and ten thousand at thy right hand; but it shall not come nigh thee.

Only with thine eyes shalt thou behold and see the reward of the wicked.

Because thou hast made the Lord, which is my refuge, even the most High, thy habitation;

There shall no evil befall thee, neither shall any plague come nigh thy dwelling.

Psalms 91:1-10

Bow down thine ear, O Lord, hear me: for I am poor and needy.

Preserve my soul; for I am holy: O thou my God, save thy servant that trusteth in thee.

Be merciful unto me, O Lord: for I cry unto thee daily.

Rejoice the soul of thy servant: for unto thee, O Lord, do I lift up my soul.

For thou, Lord, art good, and ready to forgive; and plenteous in mercy unto all them that call upon thee.

Give ear, O Lord, unto my prayer; and attend to the voice of my supplications.

Psalms 86:1-6

Thou art my God, and I will praise thee: thou art my God, I will exalt thee.

Psalms 118:28

Trouble and anguish have taken hold on me: yet thy commandments are my delights.

The righteousness of thy testimonies is everlasting: give me understanding, and I shall live.

Psalms 119:143, 144

I cried unto thee, O Lord: I said, Thou art my refuge and my portion in the land of the living.

Attend unto my cry; for I am brought very low: deliver me from my persecutors; for they are stronger than I.

Bring my soul out of prison, that I may praise thy name; the righteous shall compass me about; for thou shalt deal bountifully with me.

Psalms 142:5-7

And I, brethren, when I came to you, came not with excellency of speech or of wisdom, declaring unto you the testimony of God.

For I determined not to know any thing among you, save Jesus Christ, and him crucified.

And I was with you in weakness, and in fear, and in much trembling.

And my speech and my preaching was not with enticing words of man's wisdom, but in demonstration of the Spirit and of power:

That your faith should not stand in the wisdom of men, but in the power of God.

I Corinthians 2:1-5

Let this mind be in you, which was also in Christ Jesus:

Who, being in the form of God, thought it not robbery to be equal with God:

But made himself of no reputation, and took upon him the form of a servant, and was made in the likeness of men:

And being found in fashion as a man, he humbled himself, and became obedient unto death, even the death of the cross.

Wherefore God also hath highly exalted him, and given him a name which is above every name:

Philippians 2:5-9

Your children disobey you

Children, obey your parents in the Lord: for this is right.

And, ye fathers, provoke not your children to wrath: but bring them up in the nurture and admonition of the Lord.

Ephesians 6:1, 4

But thou, O Lord, art a God full of compassion, and gracious, long suffering, and plenteous in mercy and truth.

O turn unto me, and have mercy upon me; give thy strength unto thy servant, and save the son of thine handmaid.

Psalms 86:15, 16

If his children forsake my law, and walk not in my judgments;

If they break my statutes, and keep not my commandments;

Then will I visit their transgression with the rod, and their iniquity with stripes.

Nevertheless my lovingkindness will I not utterly take from him, nor suffer my faithfulness to fail.

My covenant will I not break, nor alter the thing that is gone out of my lips.

Psalms 89:30-34

Though he were a Son, yet learned he obedience by the things which he suffered;

Hebrews 5:8

Like as a father pitieth his children, so the Lord pitieth them that fear him.

For he knoweth our frame; he remembereth that we are dust.

As for man, his days are as grass: as a flower of the field, so he flourisheth.

For the wind passeth over it, and it is gone; and the place thereof shall know it no more.

But the mercy of the Lord is from everlasting to everlasting upon them that fear him, and his righteousness unto children's children;

Psalms 103:13-17

We have sinned with our fathers, we have committed iniquity, we have done wickedly.

Our fathers understood not thy wonders in Egypt; they remembered not the multitude of thy mercies; but provoked him at the sea, even at the Red sea.

Nevertheless he saved them for his name's sake, that he might make his mighty power to be known.

Psalms 106:6-8

Many times did he deliver them; but they provoked him with their counsel, and were brought low for their iniquity.

Nevertheless he regarded their affliction, when he heard their cry:

And he remembered for them his covenant, and repented according to the multitude of his mercies.

Psalms 106:43-45

Even a child is known by his doings, whether his work be pure, and whether it be right.

Proverbs 20:11

The proverbs of Solomon. A wise son maketh a glad father: but a foolish son is the heaviness of his mother.

Proverbs 10:1

If ye be willing and obedient, ye shall eat the good of the land:

But if ye refuse and rebel, ye shall be devoured with the sword: for the mouth of the Lord hath spoken it.

Isaiah 1:19, 20

Obey them that have the rule over you, and submit yourselves: for they watch for your souls, as they that must give account, that they may do it with joy, and not with grief: for that is unprofitable for you.

Hebrews 13:17

And Samuel said, Hath the Lord as great delight in burnt offerings and sacrifices, as in obeying the voice of the Lord? Behold, to obey is better than sacrifice, and to hearken than the fat of rams.

For rebellion is as the sin of witchcraft, and stubbornness is as iniquity and idolatry. Because thou hast rejected the word of the Lord, he hath also rejected thee from being king.

I Samuel 15:22, 23

Foolishness is bound in the heart of a child; but the rod of correction shall drive it far from him.

Proverbs 22:15

A wise son heareth his father's instruction: but a scorner heareth not rebuke.

Proverbs 13:1

Likewise, ye younger, submit yourselves unto the elder. Yea, all of you be subject one to another, and be clothed with humility: for God resisteth the proud, and giveth grace to the humble.

Humble yourselves therefore under the mighty hand of God, that he may exalt you in due time:

I Peter 5:5, 6

A member of your family dies

He healeth the broken in heart, and bindeth up their wounds.

He telleth the number of the stars; he calleth them all by their names.

Great is our Lord, and of great power: his understanding is infinite.

Psalms 147:3-5

But I would not have you to be ignorant, brethren, concerning them which are asleep, that ye sorrow not, even as others which have no hope.

For if we believe that Jesus died and rose again, even so them also which sleep in Jesus will God bring with him.

For this we say unto you by the word of the Lord, that we which are alive and remain unto the coming of the Lord shall not prevent them which are asleep.

For the Lord himself shall descend from heaven with a shout, with the voice of the archangel, and with the trump of God: and the dead in Christ shall rise first:

I Thessalonians 4:13-16

For if the dead rise not, then is not Christ raised:

And if Christ be not raised, your faith is vain; ye are yet in your sins.

Then they also which are fallen asleep in Christ are perished.

If in this life only we have hope in Christ, we are of all men most miserable.

But now is Christ risen from the dead, and become the firstfruits of them that slept.

For since by man came death, by man came also the resurrection of the dead.

For as in Adam all die, even so in Christ shall all be made alive.

But every man in his own order: Christ the firstfruits; afterward they that are Christ's at his coming.

Then cometh the end, when he shall have delivered up the kingdom to God, even the Father; when he shall have put down all rule and all authority and power.

For he must reign, till he hath put all enemies under his feet.

The last enemy that shall be destroyed is death.

I Corinthians 15:16-26

Thy kingdom is an everlasting kingdom, and thy dominion endureth throughout all generations.

The Lord upholdeth all that fall, and raiseth up all those that be bowed down.

Psalms 145:13, 14

To every thing there is a season, and a time to every purpose under the heaven:

A time to be born, and a time to die; a time to plant, and a time to pluck up that which is planted;

A time to kill, and a time to heal; a time to break down, and a time to build up;

A time to weep, and a time to laugh; a time to mourn, and a time to dance;

A time to cast away stones, and a time to gather stones together; a time to embrace, and a time to refrain from embracing;

A time to get, and a time to lose; a time to keep, and a time to cast away;

A time to rend, and a time to sew; a time to keep silence, and a time to speak;

A time to love, and a time to hate; a time of war, and a time of peace.

Ecclesiastes 3:1-8

Anger threatens your home's peace

Behold, how good and how pleasant it is for brethren to dwell together in unity!

It is like the precious ointment upon the head, that ran down upon the beard, even Aaron's beard: that went down to the skirts of his garments;

Psalms 133:1, 2

He that is slow to wrath is of great understanding: but he that is hasty of spirit exalteth folly.

Proverbs 14:29

Better is a dinner of herbs where love is, than a stalled ox and hatred therewith.

A wrathful man stirreth up strife: but he that is slow to anger appeaseth strife.

Proverbs 15:17, 18

I am for peace: but when I speak, they are for war.

I will lift up mine eyes unto the hills, from whence cometh my help.

My help cometh from the Lord, which made heaven and earth.

He will not suffer thy foot to be moved: he that keepeth thee will not slumber.

Psalms 120:7, 121:1-3

He that is slow to anger is better than the mighty; and he that ruleth his spirit than he that taketh a city.

Proverbs 16:32

The beginning of strife is as when one letteth out water: therefore leave off contention, before it be meddled with.

Proverbs 17:14

For God is not the author of confusion, but of peace, as in all churches of the saints.

I Corinthians 14:33

Wherefore, my beloved brethren, let every man be swift to hear, slow to speak, slow to wrath:
For the wrath of man worketh not the righteousness of God.

James 1:19, 20

Be ye angry, and sin not: let not the sun go down upon your wrath:

Ephesians 4:26

Hear my prayer, O Lord, and let my cry come unto thee.
Hide not thy face from me in the day when I am in trouble; incline thine ear unto me: in the day when I call answer me speedily.
For my days are consumed like smoke, and my bones are burned as an hearth.
My heart is smitten, and withered like grass; so that I forget to eat my bread.

Psalms 102:1-4

But thou, O Lord, shalt endure for ever; and thy remembrance unto all generations.

Psalms 102:12

Let your speech be alway with grace, seasoned with salt, that ye may know how ye ought to answer every man.

Colossians 4:6

Whoso keepeth his mouth and his tongue keepeth his soul from troubles.

Proverbs 21:23

Pleasant words are as an honeycomb, sweet to the soul, and health to the bones.

Proverbs 16:24

Now I beseech you, brethren, by the name of our Lord Jesus Christ, that ye all speak the same thing, and that there be no divisions among you; but that ye be perfectly joined together in the same mind and in the same judgment.

I Corinthians 1:10

Your family grows apart

God setteth the solitary in families: he bringeth out those which are bound with chains: but the rebellious dwell in a dry land.

Psalms 68:6

Children's children are the crown of old men; and the glory of children are their fathers.
Proverbs 17:6

Therefore is my spirit overwhelmed within me; my heart within me is desolate.

I remember the days of old; I meditate on all thy works; I muse on the work of thy hands.

I stretch forth my hands unto thee: my soul thirsteth after thee, as a thirsty land. Selah.

Hear me speedily, O Lord: my spirit faileth: hide not thy face from me, lest I be like unto them that go down into the pit.

Cause me to hear thy lovingkindness in the morning; for in thee do I trust: cause me to know the way wherein I should walk; for I lift up my soul unto thee.

Psalms 143:4-8

He that handleth a matter wisely shall find good; and whoso trusteth in the Lord, happy is he.
Proverbs 16:20

A merry heart maketh a cheerful countenance: but by sorrow of the heart the spirit is broken.

The heart of him that hath understanding seeketh knowledge: but the mouth of fools feedeth on foolishness.

All the days of the afflicted are evil: but he that is of a merry heart hath a continual feast.

Better is little with the fear of the Lord than great treasure and trouble therewith.

Proverbs 15:13-16

Every wise woman buildeth her house: but the foolish plucketh it down with her hands.

Proverbs 14:1

And I, brethren, could not speak unto you as unto spiritual, but as unto carnal, even as unto babes in Christ.

I have fed you with milk, and not with meat: for hitherto ye were not able to bear it, neither yet now are ye able.

For ye are yet carnal: for whereas there is among you envying, and strife, and divisions, are ye not carnal, and walk as men?

I Corinthians 3:1-3

For by one Spirit are we all baptized into one body, whether we be Jews or Gentiles, whether we be bond or free; and have been all made to drink into one Spirit.

For the body is not one member but many.

If the foot shall say, Because I am not the hand, I am not of the body; is it therefore not of the body?

And if the ear shall say, Because I am not the eye, I am not of the body; is it therefore not of the body?

If the whole body were an eye, where were the hearing? If the whole were hearing, where were the smelling?

But now hath God set the members every one of them in the body, as it hath pleased him.

And if they were all one member, where were the body?

But now are they many members, yet but one body.

And the eye cannot say unto the hand, I have no need of thee: nor again the head to the feet, I have no need of you.

Nay, much more those members of the body, which seem to be more feeble, are necessary:

And those members of the body, which we think to be less honourable, upon these we bestow more abundant honour; and our uncomely parts have more abundant comeliness.

For our comely parts have no need: but God hath tempered the body together, having given more abundant honour to that part which lacked:

That there should be no schism in the body; but that the members should have the same care one for another.

And whether one member suffer, all the members suffer with it; or one member be honoured, all the members rejoice with it.

I Corinthians 12:13-26

And Jesus knew their thoughts, and said unto them, Every kingdom divided against itself is brought to desolation; and every city or house divided against itself shall not stand:

Matthew 12:25

A brother offended is harder to be won than a strong city: and their contentions are like the bars of a castle.

Proverbs 18:19

A merry heart doeth good like a medicine: but a broken spirit drieth the bones.

Proverbs 17:22

Better is a dry morsel, and quietness therewith, than an house full of sacrifices with strife.

Proverbs 17:1

Follow peace with all men, and holincss, without which no man shall see the Lord:

Looking diligently lest any man fail of the grace of God; lest any root of bitterness springing up trouble you, and thereby many be defiled;

Hebrews 12:14, 15

God Protects You When...

You are concerned about the world's influence on your children

My son, keep thy father's commandment, and forsake not the law of thy mother:

Bind them continually upon thine heart, and tie them about thy neck.

When thou goest, it shall lead thee; when thou sleepest, it shall keep thee; and when thou awakest, it shall talk with thee.

For the commandment is a lamp; and the law is light; and reproofs of instruction are the way of life:

Proverbs 6:20-23

Train up a child in the way he should go: and when he is old, he will not depart from it.

Proverbs 22:6

Whoso keepeth the law is a wise son: but he that is a companion of riotous men shameth his father.

Proverbs 28:7

And when he had called the people unto him with his disciples also, he said unto them, Whosoever will come after me, let him deny himself, and take up his cross, and follow me.

For whosoever will save his life shall lose it; but whosoever shall lose his life for my sake and the gospel's, the same shall save it.

For what shall it profit a man, if he shall gain the whole world, and lose his own soul?

Mark 8:34-36

I beseech you therefore, brethren, by the mercies of God, that ye present you bodies a living sacrifice, holy, acceptable unto God, which is your reasonable service.

And be not conformed to this world: but be ye transformed by the renewing of your mind, that ye may prove what is that good, and acceptable, and perfect, will of God.

Romans 12:1, 2

Be ye not unequally yoked together with unbelievers: for what fellowship hath righteousness with unrighteousness? and what communion hath light with darkness?

And what concord hath Christ with Belial? or what part hath he that believeth with an infidel?

And what agreement hath the temple of God with idols? for ye are the temple of the living God; as God hath said, I will dwell in them, and walk in them; and I will be their God, and they shall be my people.

Wherefore come out from among them, and be ye separate, saith the Lord, and touch not the unclean thing; and I will receive you,

And will be a Father unto you, and ye shall be my sons and daughters, saith the Lord Almighty.

II Corinthians 6:14-18

For the unbelieving husband is sanctified by the wife, and the unbelieving wife is sanctified by the husband: else were your children unclean; but now are they holy.

I Corinthians 7:14

Deliver thyself as a roe from the hand of the hunter, and as a bird from the hand of the fowler.

Go to the ant, thou sluggard; consider her ways, and be wise:

Which having no guide, overseer, or ruler,

Provideth her meat in the summer, and gathereth her food in the harvest.

How long wilt thou sleep, O sluggard? when wilt thou arise out of thy sleep?

Yet a little sleep, a little slumber, a little folding of the hands to sleep:

So shall thy poverty come as one that travelleth, and thy want as an armed man.

Proverbs 6:5-11

Let no man deceive you with vain words: for because of these things cometh the wrath of God upon the children of disobedience.

Be not ye therefore partakers with them.

For ye were sometimes darkness, but now are ye light in the Lord: walk as children of light:

(For the fruit of the Spirit is in all goodness and righteousness and truth;)

Proving what is acceptable unto the Lord.

And have no fellowship with the unfruitful works of darkness, but rather reprove them.

For it is a shame even to speak of those things which are done of them in secret.

Ephesians 5:6-12

Beware of false prophets, which come to you in sheep's clothing, but inwardly they are ravening wolves.

Ye shall know them by their fruits. Do men gather grapes of thorns, or figs of thistles?

Even so every good tree bringeth forth good fruit; but a corrupt tree bringeth forth evil fruit.

Matthew 7:15-17

So shall my word be that goeth forth out of my mouth: it shall not return unto me void, but it shall accomplish that which I please, and it shall prosper in the thing whereto I sent it.

For ye shall go out with joy, and be led forth with peace: the mountains and the hills shall break forth before you into singing, and all the trees of the field shall clap their hands.

Instead of the thorn shall come up the fir tree, and instead of the brier shall come up the myrtle tree: and it shall be to the Lord for a name, for an everlasting sign that shall not be cutoff.

Isaiah 55:11-13

There hath no temptation taken you but such as is common to man: but God is faithful, who will not suffer you to be tempted above that ye are able; but will with the temptation also make a way to escape, that ye may be able to bear it.

I Corinthians 10:13

You don't know what decisions are best for your family

The steps of a good man are ordered by the Lord: and he delighteth in his way.

Though he fall, he shall not be utterly cast down: for the Lord upholdeth him with his hand.

Psalms 37:23, 24

And all thy children shall be taught of the Lord; and great shall be the peace of thy children.

Isaiah 54:13

And though the Lord give you the bread of adversity, and the water of affliction, yet shall not thy teachers be removed into a corner any more, but thine eyes shall see thy teachers:

And thine ears shall hear a word behind thee, saying, This is the way, walk ye in it, when ye turn to the right hand, and when ye turn to the left.

Isaiah 30:20, 21

Bow down thine ear, and hear the words of the wise, and apply thine heart unto my knowledge.

For it is a pleasant thing if thou keep them within thee; they shall withal be fitted in thy lips.

Proverbs 22:17, 18

Now therefore fear the Lord, and serve him in sincerity and in truth: and put away the gods which your fathers served on the other side of the flood, and in Egypt; and serve ye the Lord.

And if it seem evil unto you to serve the Lord, choose you this day whom ye will serve; whether the gods which your fathers served that were on the other side of the flood, or the gods of the Amorites, in whose land ye dwell: but as for me and my house, we will serve the Lord.

And the people answered and said, God forbid that we should forsake the Lord, to serve other gods;

Joshua 24:14-16

And the Lord shall guide thee continually, and satisfy thy soul in drought, and make fat thy bones: and thou shalt be like a watered garden, and like a spring of water, whose waters fail not.

And they that shall be of thee shall build the old waste places: thou shalt raise up the foundations of many generations; and thou shalt be called, The repairer of the breach, The restorer of paths to dwell in.

Isaiah 58:11, 12

Thou hast dealt well with thy servant, O Lord, according unto thy word.

Teach me good judgment and knowledge: for I have believed thy commandments.

Psalms 119:65, 66

So foolish was I, and ignorant: I was as a beast before thee.

Nevertheless I am continually with thee: thou hast holden me by my right hand.

Thou shalt guide me with thy counsel, and afterward receive me to glory.

Whom have I in heaven but thee? and there is none upon earth that I desire beside thee.

My flesh and my heart faileth: but God is the strength of my heart, and my portion for ever.

Psalms 73:22-26

Thou gavest also thy good spirit to instruct them, and withheldest not thy manna from their mouth, and gavest them water for their thirst.

Nehemiah 9:20

Do all things without murmurings and disputings:

That ye may be blameless and harmless, the sons of God, without rebuke, in the midst of a crooked and perverse nation, among whom ye shine as lights in the world;

Holding forth the word of life; that I may rejoice in the day of Christ, that I have not run in vain, neither laboured in vain.

Philippians 2:14-16

Trust in the Lord with all thine heart; and lean not unto thine own understanding.

In all thy ways acknowledge him, and he shall direct thy paths.

Proverbs 3:5, 6

Hearken unto me, O Jacob and Israel, my called; I am he; I am the first, I also am the last.

Mine hand also hath laid the foundation of the earth, and my right hand hath spanned the heavens: when I call unto them, they stand up together.

Come ye near unto me, hear ye this; I have not spoken in secret from the beginning; from the time that it was, there am I: and now the Lord God, and his Spirit, hath sent me.

Thus saith the Lord, thy Redeemer, the Holy One of Israel; I am the Lord thy God which teacheth thee to profit, which leadeth thee by the way that thou shouldest go.

Isaiah 48:12, 13, 16, 17

You question God's power to meet all situations

Behold, happy is the man whom God correcteth: therefore despise not thou the chastening of the Almighty:

For he maketh sore, and bindeth up: he woundeth, and his hands make whole.

He shall deliver thee in six troubles: yea, in seven there shall no evil touch thee.

In famine he shall redeem thee from death: and in war from the power of the sword.

Thou shalt be hid from the scourge of the tongue: neither shalt thou be afraid of destruction when it cometh.

At destruction and famine thou shalt laugh: neither shalt thou be afraid of the beasts of the earth.

For thou shalt be in league with the stones of the field: and the beasts of the field shall be at peace with thee.

And thou shalt know that thy tabernacle shall be in peace; and thou shalt visit thy habitation, and shalt not sin.

Thou shalt know also that thy seed shall be great, and thine offspring as the grass of the earth.

Thou shalt come to thy grave in a full age, like as a shock of corn cometh in in his season.

Lo this, we have searched it, so it is; hear it, and know thou it for thy good.

Job 5:17-27

For our gospel came not unto you in word only, but also in power, and in the Holy Ghost, and in much assurance; as ye know what manner of men we were among you for your sake.

I Thessalonians 1:5

And the very God of peace sanctify you wholly; and I pray God your whole spirit and soul and body be preserved blameless unto the coming of our Lord Jesus Christ.

Faithful is he that calleth you, who also will do it.

I Thessalonians 5:23, 24

For this cause we also, since the day we heard it, do not cease to pray for you, and to desire that ye might be filled with the knowledge of his will in all wisdom and spiritual understanding;

That ye might walk worthy of the Lord unto all pleasing, being fruitful in every good work, and increasing in the knowledge of God;

Strengthened with all might, according to his glorious power, unto all patience and longsuffering with joyfulness;

Giving thanks unto the Father, which hath made us meet to be partakers of the inheritance of the saints in light:

Who hath delivered us from the power of darkness, and hath translated us into the kingdom of his dear Son:

Colossians 1:9-13

And the apostles said unto the Lord, Increase our faith.

And the Lord said, If ye had faith as a grain of mustard seed, ye might say unto this sycamine tree, Be thou plucked up by the root, and be thou planted in the sea; and it should obey you.

Luke 17:5, 6

And when he was entered into a ship, his disciples followed him.

And, behold, there arose a great tempest in the sea, insomuch that the ship was covered with the waves: but he was asleep.

And his disciples came to him, and awoke him, saying, Lord, save us: we perish.

And he saith unto them, Why are ye fearful, O ye of little faith? Then he arose, and rebuked the winds and the sea; and there was a great calm.

But the men marvelled, saying, What manner of man is this, that even the winds and the sea obey him!

Matthew 8:23-27

Wherefore I also, after I heard of your faith in the Lord Jesus, and love unto all the saints,

Cease not to give thanks for you, making mention of you in my prayers;

That the God of our Lord Jesus Christ, the Father of glory, may give unto you the spirit of wisdom and revelation in the knowledge of him:

The eyes of your understanding being enlightened; that ye may know what is the hope of his calling, and what the riches of the glory of his inheritance in the saints,

And what is the exceeding greatness of his power to us-ward who believe, according to the working of his mighty power,

Which he wrought in Christ, when he raised him from the dead, and set him at his own right hand in the heavenly places,

Far above all principality, and power, and might, and dominion, and every name that is named, not only in this world, but also in that which is to come:

And hath put all things under his feet, and gave him to be the head over all things to the church,

Which is his body, the fulness of him that filleth all in all.

Ephesians 1:15-23

You feel depressed and lose your way

Now faith is the substance of things hoped for, the evidence of things not seen.

For by it the elders obtained a good report.

Through faith we understand that the worlds were framed by the word of God, so that things which are seen were not made of things which do appear.

These all died in faith, not having received the promises, but having seen them afar off, and were persuaded of them, and embraced them, and confessed that they were strangers and pilgrims on the earth.

Hebrews 11:1-3, 13

The Lord knoweth how to deliver the godly out of temptations, and to reserve the unjust unto the day of judgment to be punished:

II Peter 2:9

For ye have need of patience, that, after ye have done the will of God, ye might receive the promise.

For yet a little while, and he that shall come will come, and will not tarry.

Hebrews 10:36, 37

Ye have not yet resisted unto blood, striving against sin.

And ye have forgotten the exhortation which speaketh unto you as unto children, My son, despise not thou the chastening of the Lord, nor faint when thou art rebuked of him:

For whom the Lord loveth he chasteneth, and scourgeth every son whom he receiveth.

Hebrews 12:4-6

Whosoever shall seek to save his life shall lose it; and whosoever shall lose his life shall preserve it.

Luke 17:33

Nevertheless he saved them for his name's sake, that he might make his mighty power to be known.

Psalms 106:8

So that we may boldly say, The Lord is my helper, and I will not fear what man shall do unto me.

Hebrews 13:6

Submit yourselves therefore to God. Resist the devil, and he will flee from you.

Draw nigh to God, and he will draw nigh to you. Cleanse your hands, ye sinners; and purify your hearts, ye double minded.

Be afflicted, and mourn, and weep: let your laughter be turned to mourning, and your joy to heaviness.

Humble yourselves in the sight of the Lord, and he shall lift you up.

James 4:7-10

Blessed is the man that endureth temptation: for when he is tried, he shall receive the crown of life, which the Lord hath promised to them that love him.

Let no man say when he is tempted, I am tempted of God: for God cannot be tempted with evil, neither tempteth he any man:

But every man is tempted, when he is drawn away of his own lust, and enticed.

Then when lust hath conceived, it bringeth forth sin: and sin, when it is finished, bringeth forth death.

Do not err, my beloved brethren.

James 1:12-16

Yet if any man suffer as a Christian, let him not be ashamed; but let him glorify God on this behalf.

Wherefore let them that suffer according to the will of God commit the keeping of their souls to him in well doing, as unto a faithful Creator.

I Peter 4:16, 19

Having a good conscience; that, whereas they speak evil of you, as of evildoers, they may be ashamed that falsely accuse your good conversation in Christ.

For it is better, if the will of God be so, that ye suffer for well doing, than for evil doing.

For Christ also hath once suffered for sins, the just for the unjust, that he might bring us to God, being put to death in the flesh, but quickened by the Spirit:

I Peter 3:16-18

My little children, these things write I unto you, that ye sin not. And if any man sin, we have an advocate with the Father, Jesus Christ the righteous:

And he is the propitiation for our sins: and not for ours only, but also for the sins of the whole world.

I John 2:1, 2

God Challenges You To...

Teach your children to love God

I write unto you, little children, because your sins are forgiven you for his name's sake.

I write unto you, fathers, because ye have known him that is from the beginning. I write unto you, young men, because ye have overcome the wicked one. I write unto you, little children, because ye have known the Father.

I have written unto you, fathers, because ye have known him that is from the beginning. I have written unto you, young men, because ye are strong, and the word of God abideth in you, and ye have overcome the wicked one.

Love not the world, neither the things that are in the world. If any man love the world, the love of the Father is not in him.

For all that is in the world, the lust of the flesh, and the lust of the eyes, and the pride of life, is not of the Father, but is of the world.

And the world passeth away, and the lust thereof: but he that doeth the will of God abideth for ever.

I John 2:12-17

Beloved, let us love one another: for love is of God; and every one that loveth is born of God, and knoweth God.

He that loveth not knoweth not God; for God is love.

In this was manifested the love of God toward us, because that God sent his only begotten Son into the world, that we might live through him.

Herein is love, not that we loved God, but that he loved us, and sent his Son to be the propitiation for our sins.

Beloved, if God so loved us, we ought also to love one another.

No man hath seen God at any time. If we love one another, God dwelleth in us, and his love is perfected in us.

Hereby know we that we dwell in him, and he in us, because he hath given us of his Spirit.

And we have seen and do testify that the Father sent the Son to be the Saviour of the world.

Whosoever shall confess that Jesus is the Son of God, God dwelleth in him, and he in God.

And we have known and believed the love that God hath to us. God is love; and he that dwelleth in love dwelleth in God, and God in him.

Herein is our love made perfect, that we may have boldness in the day of judgment: because as he is, so are we in this world.

There is no fear in love; but perfect love casteth out fear: because fear hath torment. He that feareth is not made perfect in love.

We love him, because he first loved us.

If a man say, I love God, and hateth his brother, he is a liar: for he that loveth not his brother whom he hath seen, how can he love God whom he hath not seen?

And this commandment have we from him, That he who loveth God love his brother also.

I John 4:7-21

Then were there brought unto him little children, that he should put his hands on them, and pray: and the disciples rebuked them.

But Jesus said, Suffer little children, and forbid them not, to come unto me: for of such is the kingdom of heaven.

And he laid his hands on them, and departed thence.

Matthew 19:13-15

He came unto his own, and his own received him not.

But as many as received him, to them gave he power to become the sons of God, even to them that believe on his name:

John 1:11, 12

Jesus answered and said unto him, Verily, verily, I say unto thee, Except a man be born again, he cannot see the kingdom of God.

Nicodemus saith unto him, How can a man be born when he is old? can he enter the second time into his mother's womb, and be born?

Jesus answered, Verily, verily, I say unto thee, Except a man be born of water and of the Spirit, he cannot enter into the kingdom of God.

That which is born of the flesh is flesh; and that which is born of the Spirit is spirit.

Marvel not that I said unto thee, Ye must be born again.

John 3:3-7

Grow in your own Christian walk

The elder unto the wellbeloved Gaius, whom I love in the truth.

Beloved, I wish above all things that thou mayest prosper and be in health, even as thy soul prospereth.

For I rejoiced greatly, when the brethren came and testified of the truth that is in thee, even as thou walkest in the truth.

I have no greater joy than to hear that my children walk in truth.

III John 1-4

Teach me, O Lord, the way of thy statutes; and I shall keep it unto the end.

Give me understanding, and I shall keep thy law; yea, I shall observe it with my whole heart.

Make me to go in the path of thy commandments; for therein do I delight.

Psalms 119:33-35

And hereby we do know that we know him, if we keep his commandments.

He that saith, I know him, and keepeth not his commandments, is a liar, and the truth is not in him.

But whoso keepeth his word, in him verily is the love of God perfected: hereby know we that we are in him.

He that saith he abideth in him ought himself also so to walk, even as he walked.

I John 2:3-6

Thy word is a lamp unto my feet, and a light unto my path.

I have sworn, and I will perform it, that I will keep thy righteous judgments.

I am afflicted very much: quicken me, O Lord, according unto thy word.

Accept, I beseech thee, the freewill offerings of my mouth, O Lord, and teach me thy judgments.

My soul is continually in my hand: yet do I not forget thy law.

Psalms 119:105-109

Having therefore these promises, dearly beloved, let us cleanse ourselves from all filthiness of the flesh and spirit, perfecting holiness in the fear of God.

II Corinthians 7:1

Apply thine heart unto instruction, and thine ears to the words of knowledge.

Proverbs 23:12

Teach me thy way, O Lord; I will walk in thy truth: unite my heart to fear thy name.

I will praise thee, O Lord my God, with all my heart: and I will glorify thy name for evermore.

Psalms 86:11, 12

Because it is written, Be ye holy; for I am holy.

I Peter 1:16

Ye cannot drink the cup of the Lord, and the cup of devils: ye cannot be partakers of the Lord's table, and of the table of devils.

Do we provoke the Lord to jealousy? are we stronger than he?

All things are lawful for me, but all things are not expedient: all things are lawful for me, but all things edify not.

I Corinthians 10:21-23

That the righteousness of the law might be fulfilled in us, who walk not after the flesh, but after the Spirit.

For they that are after the flesh do mind the things of the flesh; but they that are after the Spirit the things of the Spirit.

For to be carnally minded is death; but to be spiritually minded is life and peace.

Romans 8:4-6

Two men went up into the temple to pray; the one a Pharisee, and the other a publican.

The Pharisee stood and prayed thus with himself, God, I thank thee, that I am not as other men are, extortioners, unjust, adulterers, or even as this publican.

I fast twice in the week, I give tithes of all that I possess.

And the publican, standing afar off, would not lift up so much as his eyes unto heaven, but smote upon his breast, saying, God be merciful to me a sinner.

I tell you, this man went down to his house justified rather than the other: for every one that exalteth himself shall be abased; and he that humbleth himself shall be exalted.

Luke 18:10-14

And that, knowing the time, that now it is high time to awake out of sleep: for now is our salvation nearer than when we believed.

The night is far spent, the day is at hand: let us therefore cast off the works of darkness, and let us put on the armour of light.

Let us walk honestly, as in the day; not in rioting and drunkenness, not in chambering and wantonness, not in strife and envying.

But put ye on the Lord Jesus Christ, and make not provision for the flesh, to fulfil the lusts thereof.

Romans 13:11-14

Fight the good fight of faith, lay hold on eternal life, whereunto thou art also called, and hast professed a good profession before many witnesses.

I Timothy 6:12

Whosoever believeth that Jesus is the Christ is born of God: and every one that loveth him that begat loveth him also that is begotten of him.

By this we know that we love the children of God, when we love God, and keep his commandments:

For this is the love of God, that we keep his commandments: and his commandments are not grievous.

I John 5:1-3

Share your faith with your children

And Jesus called a little child unto him, and set him in the midst of them,

And said, Verily I say unto you, Except ye be converted, and become as little children, ye shall not enter into the kingdom of heaven.

Whosoever therefore shall humble himself as this little child, the same is greatest in the kingdom of heaven.

And whoso shall receive one such little child in my name receiveth me.

But whoso shall offend one of these little ones which believe in me, it were better for him that a millstone were hanged about his neck, and that he were drowned in the depth of the sea.

Take heed that ye despise not one of these little ones; for I say unto you, That in heaven their angels do always behold the face of my Father which is in heaven.

For the Son of man is come to save that which was lost.

How think ye? if a man have an hundred sheep, and one of them be gone astray, doth he not leave the ninety and nine, and goeth into the mountains, and seeketh that which is gone astray?

And if so be that he find it, verily I say unto you, he rejoiceth more of that sheep, than of the ninety and nine which went not astray.

Even so it is not the will of your Father which is in heaven, that one of these little ones should perish.

Matthew 18:2-6, 10-14

And these words, which I command thee this day, shall be in thine heart:

And thou shalt teach them diligently unto thy children, and shalt talk of them when thou sittest in thine house, and when thou walkest by the way, and when thou liest down, and when thou risest up.

And thou shalt bind them for a sign upon thine hand, and they shall be as frontlets between thine eyes.

And thou shalt write them upon the posts of thy house, and on thy gates.

Deuteronomy 6:6-9

But before faith came, we were kept under the law, shut up unto the faith which should afterwards be revealed.

Wherefore the law was our schoolmaster to bring us unto Christ, that we might be justified by faith.

But after that faith is come, we are no longer under a schoolmaster.

For ye are all the children of God by faith in Christ Jesus.

For as many of you as have been baptized into Christ have put on Christ.

Galatians 3:23-27

But what saith it? The word is nigh thee, even in thy mouth, and in thy heart: that is, the word of faith, which we preach;

That if thou shalt confess with thy mouth the Lord Jesus, and shalt believe in thine heart that God hath raised him from the dead, thou shalt be saved.

For with the heart man believeth unto righteousness; and with the mouth confession is made unto salvation.

For the scripture saith, Whosoever believeth on him shall not be ashamed.

Romans 10:8-11

For this is good and acceptable in the sight of God our Saviour;

Who will have all men to be saved, and to come unto the knowledge of the truth.

1 Timothy 2:3, 4

Brethren, if any of you do err from the truth, and one convert him;

Let him know, that he which converteth the sinner from the error of his way, shall save a soul from death, and shall hide a multitude of sins.

James 5:19, 20

For the perfecting of the saints, for the work of the ministry, for the edifying of the body of Christ:

Till we all come in the unity of the faith, and of the knowledge of the Son of God, unto a perfect man, unto the measure of the stature of the fulness of Christ:

That we henceforth be no more children, tossed to and fro, and carried about with every wind of doctrine, by the sleight of men, and cunning craftiness, whereby they lie in wait to deceive;

But speaking the truth in love, may grow up into him in all things, which is the head, even Christ:

Ephesians 4:12-15

And the keeper of the prison awaking out of his sleep, and seeing the prison doors open, he drew out his sword, and would have killed himself, supposing that the prisoners had been fled.

But Paul cried with a loud voice, saying, Do thyself no harm: for we are all here.

Then he called for a light, and sprang in, and came trembling, and fell down before Paul and Silas,

And brought them out, and said, Sirs, what must I do to be saved?

And they said, Believe on the Lord Jesus Christ, and thou shalt be saved, and thy house.

And they spake unto him the word of the Lord, and to all that were in his house.

And he took them the same hour of the night, and washed their stripes; and was baptized, he and all his, straightway.

Acts 16:27-33

And they brought young children to him, that he should touch them: and his disciples rebuked those that brought them.

But when Jesus saw it, he was much displeased, and said unto them, Suffer the little children to come unto me, and forbid them not: for of such is the kingdom of God.

Verily I say unto you, Whosoever shall not receive the kingdom of God as a little child, he shall not enter therein.

And he took them up in his arms, put his hands upon them, and blessed them.

Mark 10:13-16

Deal honestly with those close to you

The fathers have eaten a sour grape, and the children's teeth are set on edge.

Jeremiah 31:29b

Judge not, that ye be not judged.

For with what judgment ye judge, ye shall be judged: and with what measure ye mete, it shall be measured to you again.

And why beholdest thou the mote that is in thy brother's eye, but considerest not the beam that is in thine own eye?

Or how wilt thou say to thy brother, Let me pull out the mote out of thine eye; and, behold, a beam is in thine own eye?

Thou hypocrite, first cast out the beam out of thine own eye; and then shalt thou see clearly to cast out the mote out of thy brother's eye.

Matthew 7:1-5

Lie not one to another, seeing that ye have put off the old man with his deeds;

And have put on the new man, which is renewed in knowledge after the image of him that created him:

Colossians 3:9, 10

Withhold not good from them to whom it is due, when it is in the power of thine hand to do it.

Proverbs 3:27

He that being often reproved hardeneth his neck, shall suddenly be destroyed, and that without remedy.

Proverbs 29:1

Lying lips are abomination to the Lord: but they that deal truly are his delight.

Proverbs 12:22

And the Lord sent Nathan unto David. And he came unto him, and said unto him, There were two men in one city; the one rich, and the other poor.

The rich man had exceeding many flocks and herds:

But the poor man had nothing, save one little ewe lamb, which he had bought and nourished up: and it grew up together with him, and with his children; it did eat of his own meat, and drank of his own cup, and lay in his bosom, and was unto him as a daughter.

And there came a traveller unto the rich man, and he spared to take of his own flock and of his own herd, to dress for the wayfaring man that was come unto him; but took the poor man's lamb, and dressed it for the man that was come to him.

And David's anger was greatly kindled against the man; and he said to Nathan, As the Lord liveth, the man that hath done this thing shall surely die:

And he shall restore the lamb fourfold, because he did this thing, and because he had no pity.

And Nathan said to David, Thou art the man.

II Samuel 12:1-7a

And take not the word of truth utterly out of my mouth; for I have hoped in thy judgments.

So shall I keep thy law continually for ever and ever.

And I will walk at liberty: for I seek thy precepts.

Psalms 119:43-45

If so be that ye have heard him, and have been taught by him, as the truth is in Jesus:

That ye put off concerning the former conversation the old man, which is corrupt according to the deceitful lusts;

And be renewed in the spirit of your mind;

And that ye put on the new man, which after God is created in righteousness and true holiness.

Wherefore putting away lying, speak every man truth with his neighbour: for we are members one of another.

Ephesians 4:21-25

Ask forgiveness when you wrong your family

And he shall turn the heart of the fathers to the children, and the heart of the children to their fathers, lest I come and smite the earth with a curse.

Malachi 4:6

He that covereth his sins shall not prosper: but whoso confesseth and forsaketh them shall have mercy.

Proverbs 28:13

A man's pride shall bring him low: but honour shall uphold the humble in spirit.

Proverbs 29:23

Take heed to yourselves: If thy brother trespass against thee, rebuke him; and if he repent, forgive him.

And if he trespass against thee seven times in a day turn again to thee, saying, I repent; thou shalt forgive him.

Luke 17:3, 4

And when ye stand praying, forgive, if ye have ought against any: that your Father also which is in heaven may forgive you your trespasses.

But if ye do not forgive, neither will your Father which is in heaven forgive your trespasses.

Mark 11:25, 26

The just man walketh in his integrity: his children are blessed after him.

Proverbs 20:7

I Therefore, the prisoner of the Lord, beseech you that ye walk worthy of the vocation wherewith ye are called,

With all lowliness and meekness, with longsuffering, forbearing one another in love;

Endeavouring to keep the unity of the Spirit in the bond of peace.

Ephesians 4:1-3

Forbearing one another, and forgiving one another, if any man have a quarrel against any: even as Christ forgave you, so also do ye.

Colossians 3:13

For if ye forgive men their trespasses, your heavenly Father will also forgive you:

But if ye forgive not men their trespasses, neither will your Father forgive your trespasses.

Matthew 6:14, 15

Never stop loving your wife

Live joyfully with the wife whom thou lovest all the days of the life of thy vanity, which he hath given thee under the sun, all the days of thy vanity: for that is thy portion in this life, and in thy labour which thou takest under the sun.

Ecclesiastes 9:9

Many waters cannot quench love neither can the floods drown it: if a man would give all the substance of his house for love, it would utterly be contemned.

Song of Solomon 8:7

Whoso findeth a wife findeth a good thing, and obtaineth favour of the Lord.

Proverbs 18:22

Who satisfieth thy mouth with good things; so that thy youth is renewed like the eagle's.

Psalms 103:5

Let thy fountain be blessed: and rejoice with the wife of thy youth.
Let her be as the loving hind and pleasant roe; let her breasts satisfy thee at all times; and be thou ravished always with her love.

Proverbs 5:18, 19

And he answered and said unto them, Have ye not read, that he which made them at the beginning made them male and female,

And said, For this cause shall a man leave father and mother, and shall cleave to his wife: and they twain shall be one flesh?

Wherefore they are no more twain, but one flesh. What therefore God hath joined together, let not man put asunder.

Matthew 19:4-6

How fair is thy love, my sister, my spouse! how much better is thy love than wine! and the smell of thine ointments than all spices!

Thy lips, O my spouse, drop as the honeycomb: honey and milk are under thy tongue; and the smell of thy garments is like the smell of Lebanon.

A garden inclosed is my sister, my spouse; a spring shut up, a fountain sealed.

Thy plants are an orchard of pomegranates, with pleasant fruits; camphire, with spikenard,

Spikenard and saffron; calamus and cinnamon, with all trees of frankincense; myrrh and aloes, with all the chief spices:

A fountain of gardens, a well of living waters, and streams from Lebanon.

Awake, O north wind; and come, thou south; blow upon my garden, that the spices thereof may flow out. Let my beloved come into his garden, and eat his pleasant fruits.

Song of Solomon 4:10-16

And the Lord God said, It is not good that the man should be alone; I will make him an help meet for him.

Genesis 2:18

But from the beginning of the creation God made them male and female.

For this cause shall a man leave his father and mother, and cleave to his wife;

And they twain shall be one flesh: so then they are no more twain, but one flesh.

What therefore God hath joined together, let not man put asunder.

Mark 10:6-9

Nevertheless, to avoid fornication, let every man have his own wife, and let every woman have her own husband.

Let the husband render unto the wife due benevolence: and likewise also the wife unto the husband.

The wife hath not power of her own body, but the husband: and likewise also the husband hath not power of his own body, but the wife.

Defraud ye not one the other, except it be with consent for a time, that ye may give yourselves to fasting and prayer; and come together again, that Satan tempt you not for your incontinency.

But I speak this by permission, and not of commandment.

I Corinthians 7:2-6

Marriage is honourable in all, and the bed undefiled: but whoremongers and adulterers God will judge.

Hebrews 13:4

And the Lord God caused a deep sleep to fall upon Adam, and he slept: and he took one of his ribs, and closed up the flesh instead thereof;

And the rib, which the Lord God had taken from man, made he a woman, and brought her unto the man.

And Adam said, This is now bone of my bones, and flesh of my flesh: she shall be called Woman, because she was taken out of Man.

Therefore shall a man leave his father and his mother, and shall cleave unto his wife: and they shall be one flesh.

And they were both naked, the man and his wife, and were not ashamed.

Genesis 2:21-25

House and riches are the inheritance of fathers: and a prudent wife is from the Lord.

Proverbs 19:14

GOD CHALLENGES YOU TO

Be wise with your family's finances

And it shall come to pass, if thou shalt hearken diligently unto the voice of the Lord thy God, to observe and to do all his commandments which I command thee this day, that the Lord thy God will set thee on high above all nations of the earth:

And all these blessings shall come on thee, and overtake thee, if thou shalt hearken unto the voice of the Lord thy God.

Blessed shalt thou be in the city, and blessed shalt thou be in the field.

Blessed shall be the fruit of thy body, and the fruit of thy ground, and the fruit of thy cattle, the increase of thy kine, and the flocks of thy sheep.

Blessed shall be thy basket and thy store.

Blessed shalt thou be when thou comest in, and blessed shalt thou be when thou goest out.

Deuteronomy 28:1-6

But is any provide not for his own, and specially for those of his own house, he hath denied the faith, and is worse than an infidel.

I Timothy 5:8

But thou shalt remember the Lord thy God: for it is he that giveth thee power to get wealth, that he may establish his covenant which he sware unto thy fathers, as it is this day.

Deuteronomy 8:18

If they obey and serve him, they shall spend their days in prosperity, and their years in pleasures.

Job 36:11

Trust in the Lord, and do good; so shalt thou dwell in the land, and verily thou shalt be fed.

Delight thyself also in the Lord; and he shall give thee the desires of thine heart.

Commit thy way unto the Lord; trust also in him; and he shall bring it to pass.

Psalms 37:3-5

Behold, my servant shall deal prudently, he shall be exalted and extolled, and be very high.

Isaiah 52:13

I went by the field of the slothful, and by the vineyard of the man void of understanding;

And, lo, it was all grown over with thorns, *and* nettles had covered the face thereof, and the stone wall thereof was broken down.

Then I saw, *and* considered *it* well: I looked upon *it, and* received instruction.

Yet a little sleep, a little slumber, a little folding of the hands to sleep;

So shall thy poverty come as one that travelleth; and thy want as an armed man.

Proverbs 24:30-34

The sluggard will not plow by reason of the cold; *therefore* shall he beg in harvest, and *have* nothing.

Proverbs 20:4

Better is a little with righteousness than great revenues without right.

Proverbs 16:8

For the earth is the Lord's and the fulness thereof.   *I Corinthians 10:26*

That thou appear not unto men to fast, but unto thy Father which is in secret: and thy Father, which seeth in secret, shall reward thee openly.

Lay not up for yourselves treasures upon earth, where moth and rust doth corrupt, and where rust doth corrupt, and where thieves break through and steal:

But lay up for yourselves treasures in heaven, where neither moth nor rust doth corrupt, and where thieves do not break through nor steal:

For where your treasure is, there will your heart be also.

Matthew 6:18-21

Then shalt thou prosper, if thou takest heed to fulfil the statutes and judgments which the Lord charged Moses with concerning Israel: be strong, and of good courage; dread not, nor be dismayed.

I Chronicles 22:13

For the love of money is the root of all evil: which while some coveted after, they have erred from the faith, and pierced themselves through with many sorrows.

I Timothy 6:10

The Lord maketh poor, and maketh rich: he bringeth low, and lifteth up.

He raiseth up the poor out of the dust, and lifteth up the beggar from the dunghill, to set them among princes, and to make them inherit the throne of glory: for the pillars of the earth are the Lord's, and he hath set the world upon them.

He will keep the feet of his saints, and the wicked shall be silent in darkness; for by strength shall no man prevail.

I Samuel 2:7-9

Bring your tithe into the storehouse

Honour the Lord with thy substance, and with the firstfruits of all thine increase:

So shall thy barns be filled with plenty, and thy presses shall burst out with new wine.

Proverbs 3:9, 10

The righteous shall flourish like the palm tree: he shall grow like a cedar in Lebanon.

Psalms 92:12

Give, and it shall be given unto you; good measure, pressed down, and shaken together, and running over, shall men give into your bosom. For with the same measure that ye mete withal it shall be measured to you again.

Luke 6:38

Three times in a year shall all thy males appear before the Lord thy God in the place which he shall choose; in the feast of unleavened bread, and in the feast of tabernacles: and they shall not appear before the Lord empty:

Every man shall give as he is able, according to the blessing of the Lord thy God which he hath given thee.

Deuteronomy 16:16, 17

Will a man rob God? Yet ye have robbed me. But ye say. Wherein have we robbed thee? In tithes and offerings.

Ye are cursed with a curse: for ye have robbed me, even this whole nation.

Bring ye all the tithes into the storehouse, that there may be meat in mine house, and prove me now herewith, saith the Lord of hosts, if I will not open you the windows of heaven, and pour you out a blessing, that there shall not be room enough to receive it.

And I will rebuke the devourer for your sakes, and he shall not destroy the fruits of your ground; neither shall your vine cast her fruit before the time in the field, saith the Lord of hosts.

And all nations shall call you blessed: for ye shall be a delightsome land, saith the Lord of hosts.

Malachi 3:8-12

Now concerning the collection for the saints as I have given order to the churches of Galatia, even so do ye.

Upon the first day of the week let every one of you lay by him in store, as God hath prospered him, that there be no gatherings when I come.

I Corinthians 16:1, 2

Give unto the Lord, O ye kindreds of the people, give unto the Lord glory and strength.

Give unto the Lord the glory due unto his name: bring an offering, and come into his courts.

O worship the Lord in the beauty of holiness: fear before him, all the earth.

Psalms 96:7-9

But this I say, He which soweth sparingly shall reap also sparingly; and he which soweth bountifully shall reap also bountifully.

Every man according as he purposeth in his heart, so let him give; not grudgingly, or of necessity: for God loveth a cheerful giver.

And God is able to make all grace abound toward you; that ye, always having all sufficiency in all things, may abound to every good work:

(As it is written, He hath dispersed abroad; he hath given to the poor: his righteousness remaineth for ever.

Now he that ministereth seed to the sower both minister bread for your food, and multiply your seed sown, and increase the fruits of your righteousness;)

Being enriched in every thing to all bountifulness, which causeth through us thanksgiving to God.

For the administration of this service not only supplieth the want of the saints but is abundant also by many thanksgivings unto God;

II Corinthians 9:6-12

God Listens To Your Prayers When...

Your children disappoint you

A wise servant shall have rule over a son that causeth shame, and shall have part of the inheritance among the brethren.

Proverbs 17:2

For if the firstfruit be holy, the lump is also holy: and if the root be holy, so are the branches.

Romans 11:16

(For the Lord thy God is a merciful God;) he will not forsake thee, neither destroy thee, nor forget the covenant of thy fathers which he sware unto them.

Deuteronomy 4:31

Those that be planted in the house of the Lord shall flourish in the courts of our God.

They shall still bring forth fruit in old age; they shall be fat and flourishing;

To shew that the Lord is upright: he is my rock, and there is no unrighteousness in him.

Psalms 92:13-15

Then I said, I have laboured in vain, I have spent my strength for nought, and in vain: yet surely my judgment is with the Lord, and my work with my God.

Thus saith the Lord, In an acceptable time have I heard thee, and in a day of salvation have I helped thee: and I will preserve thee, and give thee for a covenant of the people, to establish the earth, to cause to inherit the desolate heritages;

That thou mayest say to the prisoners, Go forth; to them that are in darkness, Shew yourselves. They shall feed in the ways, and their pastures shall be in all high places.

They shall not hunger nor thirst; neither shall the heat nor sun smite them: for he that hath mercy on them shall lead them, even by the springs of water shall he guide them.

And I will make all my mountains a way, and my highways shall be exalted.

Isaiah 49:4, 8-11

For I know nothing by myself; yet am I not hereby justified: but he that judgeth me is the Lord.

Therefore judge nothing before the time, until the Lord come, who both will bring to light the hidden things of darkness, and will make manifest the counsels of the hearts: and then shall every man have praise of God.

I Corinthians 4:4, 5

Who hath formed a god, or molten a graven image that is profitable for nothing?

Isaiah 44:10

He healeth the broken in heart, and bindeth up their wounds.

Psalms 147:3

Now the sons of Eli were sons of Belial; they knew not the Lord.

And the priest's custom with the people was, that, when any man offered sacrifice, the priest's servant came, while the flesh was in seething, with a fleshhook of three teeth in his hand;

Also before they burnt the fat, the priest's servant came, and said to the man that sacrificed, Give flesh to roast for the priest; for he will not have sodden flesh of thee, but raw.

And if any man said unto him, Let them not fail to burn the fat presently, and then take as much as thy soul desireth; then he would answer him, Nay; but thou shalt give it me now: and if not, I will take it by force.

Wherefore the sin of the young men was very great before the Lord: for men abhorred the offering of the Lord.

Now Eli was very old, and heard all that his sons did unto all Israel; and how they lay with the women that assembled at the door of the tabernacle of the congregation.

And he said unto them, Why do ye such things? for I hear of your evil dealings by all this people.

Nay, my sons; for it is no good report that I hear: ye make the Lord's people to transgress.

If one man sin against another, the judge shall judge him: but if a man sin against the Lord, who shall entreat for him? Notwithstanding they hearkened not unto the voice of their father, because the Lord would slay them.

I Samuel 2:12, 13, 15-17, 22-25

And, behold Cushi came; and Cushi said, Tidings, my lord the king: for the Lord hath avenged thee this day of all them that rose up against thee.

And the king said unto Cushi, Is the young man Absalom safe? And Cushi answered, The enemies of my lord the king, and all that rise against thee to do thee hurt, be as that young man is.

And the king was much moved, and went up to the chamber over the gate, and wept: and as he went, thus he said, O my son Absalom, my son, my son Absalom! would God I had died for thee, O Absalom, my son, my son!

II Samuel 18:31-33

For a small moment have I forsaken thee; but with great mercies will I gather thee.

And all thy children shall be taught of the Lord; and great shall be the peace of thy children.

Isaiah 54:7, 13

All we like sheep have gone astray; we have turned every one to his own way; and the Lord hath laid on him the iniquity of us all.

Isaiah 53:6

For the Lord will not cast off his people, neither will he forsake his inheritance.

But judgment shall return unto righteousness: and all the upright in heart shall follow it.

Psalms 94:14, 15

Therefore the redeemed of the Lord shall return, and come with singing unto Zion; and everlasting joy shall be upon their head: they shall obtain gladness and joy; and sorrow and mourning shall flee away.

Isaiah 51:11

I will not leave you comfortless: I will come to you.

John 14:18

You ask for His patience

Fathers, provoke not your children to anger, lest they be discouraged.

Colossians 3:21

Blessed is he that waiteth,

Daniel 12:12a

Better is the end of a thing than the beginning thereof: and the patient in spirit is better than the proud in spirit.

Ecclesiastes 7:8

My brethren, count it all joy when ye fall into divers temptations;

Knowing this, that the trying of your faith worketh patience.

But let patience have her perfect work, that ye may be perfect and entire, wanting nothing.

James 1:2-4

Now we exhort you, brethren, warn them that are unruly, comfort the feebleminded, support the weak, be patient toward all men.

I Thessalonians 5:14

And the servant of the Lord must not strive; but be gentle unto all men, apt to teach, patient,

II Timothy 2:24

Wherefore seeing we also are compassed about with so great a cloud of witnesses, let us lay aside every weight, and the sin which doth so easily beset us, and let us run with patience the race that is set before us.

Hebrews 12:1

For even Christ pleased not himself; but, as it is written, The reproaches of them that reproached thee fell on me.

For whatsoever things were written aforetime were written for our learning, that we through patience and comfort of the scriptures might have hope.

Now the God of patience and consolation grant you to be likeminded one toward another according to Christ Jesus:

Romans 15:3-5

And not only so, but we glory in tribulations also: knowing that tribulation worketh patience;

Romans 5:3

If there be therefore any consolation in Christ, if any comfort of love, if any fellowship of the Spirit, if any bowels and mercies,

Fulfil ye my joy, that ye be likeminded, having the same love, being of one accord, of one mind.

Let nothing be done through strife or vain glory; but in lowliness of mind let each esteem other better than themselves.

Look not every man on his own things, but every man also on the things of others.

Philippians 2:1-4

You ask for His Spirit's guidance

What shall we then say to these things? If God be for us, who can be against us?

He that spared not his own Son, but delivered him up for us all, how shall he not with him also freely give us all things?

Romans 8:31, 32

Teach me to do thy will; for thou art my God: thy spirit is good; lead me into the land of uprightness.

Quicken me, O Lord, for thy name's sake: for thy righteousness' sake bring my soul out of trouble.

Psalms 143:10, 11

Now the Lord is that Spirit: and where the Spirit of the Lord is, there is liberty.

But we all, with open face beholding as in a glass the glory of the Lord, are changed into the same image from glory to glory, even as by the Spirit of the Lord.

II Corinthians 3:17, 18

For he shall give his angels charge over thee, to keep thee in all thy ways.

They shall bear thee up in their hands, lest thou dash thy foot against a stone.

Thou shalt tread upon the lion and adder: the young lion and the dragon shalt thou trample under feet.

Because he hath set his love upon me, therefore will I deliver him: I will set him on high, because he hath known my name.

He shall call upon me, and I will answer him: I will be with him in trouble; I will deliver him, and honour him.

With long life will I satisfy him, and shew him my salvation.

Psalms 91: 11-16

Hereby know we that we dwell in him, and he is us, because he hath given us of his Spirit.
I John 4:13

This I say then, Walk in the Spirit, and ye shall not fulfil the lust of the flesh.

For the flesh lusteth against the Spirit, and the Spirit against the flesh: and these are contrary the one to the other: so that ye cannot do the things that ye would.

But if ye be led of the Spirit, ye are not under the law.

Now the works of the flesh are manifest, which are these; Adultery, fornication, uncleanness, lasciviousness,

Idolatry, witchcraft, hatred, variance, emulations, wrath, strife, seditions, heresies,

Envyings, murders, drunkenness, revellings, and such like: of the which I tell you before, as I have also told you in time past, that they which do such things shall not inherit the kingdom of God.

But the fruit of the Spirit is love, joy, peace, longsuffering, gentleness, goodness, faith,

Meekness, temperance: against such there is no law.

And they that are Christ's have crucified the flesh with the affections and lusts.

If we live in the Spirit, let us also walk in the Spirit.

Let us not be desirous of vain glory, provoking one another, envying one another.

Galatians 5:16-26

For we through the Spirit wait for the hope of righteousness by faith.

Galatians 5:5

But God hath revealed them unto us by his Spirit: for the Spirit searcheth all things, yea, the deep things of God.

For what man knoweth the things of a man, save the spirit of man which is in him? even so the things of God knoweth no man, but the Spirit of God.

Now we have received, not the spirit of the world, but the spirit which is of God; that we might know the things that are freely given to us of God.

Which things also we speak, not in the words which man's wisdom teacheth, but which the Holy Ghost teacheth; comparing spiritual things with spiritual.

But the natural man receiveth not the things of the Spirit of God: for they are foolishness unto him: neither can he know them, because they are spiritually discerned.

But he that is spiritual judgeth all things, yet he himself is judged of no man.

For who hath known the mind of the Lord, that he may instruct him? But we have the mind of Christ.

I Corinthians 2:10-16

You admit to your short-comings as a father

O God, be not far from me: O my God, make haste for my help.

My mouth shall shew forth thy righteousness and thy salvation all the day; for I know not the numbers thereof.

I will go in the strength of the Lord God: I will make mention of thy righteousness, even of thine only.

O God, thou hast taught me from my youth: and hitherto have I declared thy wondrous works.

Now also when I am old and grayheaded, O God, forsake me not; until I have shewed thy strength unto this generation, and thy power to every one that is to come.

Psalms 71:12, 15-18

Be of good courage, and he shall strengthen your heart, all ye that hope in the Lord.

Psalms 31:24

He that covereth his sins shall not prosper: but whoso confesseth and forsaketh them shall have mercy.

Proverbs 28:13

For I will pour water upon him that is thirsty, and floods upon the dry ground: I will pour my spirit upon thy seed, and my blessing upon thine offspring:

And they shall spring up as among the grass, as willows by the water courses.

Isaiah 44:3, 4

Only take heed to thyself, and keep thy soul diligently, lest thou forget the things which thine eyes have seen, and lest they depart from thy heart all the days of thy life: but teach them thy sons, and thy sons' sons:

Deuteronomy 4:9

And it shall come to pass, if thou shalt hearken diligently unto the voice of the Lord thy God, to observe and to do all his commandments which I command thee this day, that the Lord thy God will set thee on high above all nations of the earth:

Blessed shall be the fruit of thy body, and the fruit of thy ground, and the fruit of thy cattle, the increase of thy kine, and the flocks of thy sheep.

Deuteronomy 28:1, 4

So then neither is he that planteth any thing, neither he that watereth; but God that giveth the increase.

Now he that planteth and he that watereth are one: and every man shall receive his own reward according to his own labour.

For we are labourers together with God: ye are God's husbandry, ye are God's building.

I Corinthians 3:7-9

The Lord is good, a strong hold in the day of trouble; and he knoweth them that trust in him.

Nahum 1:7

For how can the servant of this my lord talk with this my lord? for as for me, straightway there remained no strength in me, neither is there breath left in me.

Then there came again and touched me one like the appearance of a man, and he strengthened me,

And said, O man greatly beloved, fear not: peace be unto thee, be strong, yea, be strong. And when he had spoken unto me, I was strengthened, and said, Let my lord speak; for thou hast strengthened me.

Then said he, Knowest thou wherefore I come unto thee? and now will I return to fight with the prince of Persia: and when I am gone forth, lo, the prince of Grecia shall come.

But I will shew thee that which is noted in the scripture of truth: and there is none that holdeth with me in these things, but Michael your prince.

Daniel 10:17-21

Call unto me, and I will answer thee, and shew thee great and mighty things, which thou knowest not.

Jeremiah 33:3

The Lord is far from the wicked: but he heareth the prayer of the righteous.

The light of the eyes rejoiceth the heart: and a good report maketh the bones fat.

The ear that heareth the reproof of life abideth among the wise.

He that refuseth instruction despiseth his own soul: but he that heareth reproof getteth understanding.

The fear of the Lord is the instruction of wisdom; and before honour is humility.

Proverbs 15:29-33

You're overwhelmed by your family responsibilities

Except the Lord build the house, they labour in vain that build it: except the Lord keep the city, the watchman waketh but in vain.

It is vain for you to rise up early, to sit up late, to eat the bread of sorrows: for so he giveth his beloved sleep.

Lo, children are an heritage of the Lord: and the fruit of the womb is his reward.

As arrows are in the hand of a mighty man; so are children of the youth.

Happy is the man that hath his quiver full of them: they shall not be ashamed, but they shall speak with the enemies in the gate.

Psalms 127:1-5

For the mountains shall depart, and the hills be removed; but my kindness shall not depart from thee, neither shall the covenant of my peace be removed, saith the Lord that hath mercy on thee.

Isaiah 54:10

I cried unto God with my voice, even unto God with my voice; and he gave ear unto me.

I remembered God, and was troubled: I complained, and my spirit was overwhelmed. Selah.

Psalms 77:1, 3

Trust in the Lord with all thine heart; and lean not unto thine own understanding.

In all thy ways acknowledge him, and he shall direct thy paths.

Be not wise in thine own eyes: fear the Lord, and depart from evil.

Proverbs 3:5-7

Lift up your eyes on high, and behold who hath created these things, that bringeth out their host by number: he calleth them all by names by the greatness of his might, for that he is strong in power; not one faileth.

Isaiah 40:26

He giveth power to the faint; and to them that have no might he increaseth strength.

Isaiah 40:29

When thou passest through the waters, I will be with thee; and through the rivers, they shall not overflow thee: when thou walkest through the fire, thou shalt not be burned; neither shall the flame kindle upon thee.

Fear not: for I am with thee: I will bring thy seed from the east, and gather thee from the west;

I will say to the north, Give up; and to the south, Keep not back: bring my sons from far, and my daughters from the ends of the earth;

Even every one that is called by my name: for I have created him for my glory, I have formed him; yea, I have made him.

Isaiah 43:2, 5-7

Be strong and of a good courage, fear not, nor be afraid of them: for the Lord thy God, he it is that doth go with thee; he will not fail thee, nor forsake thee.

Deuteronomy 31:6

Therefore, brethren, stand fast, and hold the traditions which ye have been taught, whether by word, or our epistle.

Now our Lord Jesus Christ himself, and God, even our Father, which hath loved us, and hath given us everlasting consolation and good hope through grace,

Comfort your hearts, and stablish you in every good word and work.

II Thessalonians 2:15-17

God Fills You With Joy When...

Your family gives praises to the Lord

I will extol thee, my God, O king; and I will bless thy name for ever and ever.

Every day will I bless thee; and I will praise thy name for ever and ever.

Great is the Lord, and greatly to be praised; and his greatness is unsearchable.

One generation shall praise thy works to another, and shall declare thy mighty acts.

Psalms 145:1-4

Both young men, and maidens; old men, and children:

Let them praise the name of the Lord: for his name alone is excellent; his glory is above the earth and heaven.

He also exalteth the horn of his people, the praise of all his saints; even of the child. of Israel, a people near unto him. Praise ye the Lord.

Psalms 148:12-14

Praise ye the Lord. Praise God in his sanctuary: praise him in the firmament of his power.

Praise him for his mighty acts: praise him according to his excellent greatness.

Praise him with the sound of the trumpet: praise him with the psaltery and harp.

Praise him with the timbrel and dance: praise him with stringed instruments and organs.

Praise him upon the loud cymbals: praise him upon the high sounding cymbals.

Let every thing that hath breath praise the Lord. Praise ye the Lord.

Psalms 150:1-6

This people have I formed for myself; they shall shew forth my praise.

Isaiah 43:21

I will call on the Lord, who is worthy to be praised: so shall I be saved from mine enemies.

II Samuel 22:4

Know ye that the Lord he is God: it is he that hath made us, and not we ourselves; we are his people, and the sheep of his pasture.

Enter into his gates with thanksgiving, and into his courts with praise: be thankful unto him, and bless his name.

For the Lord is good; his mercy is ever-lasting; and his truth endureth to all generations.

Psalms 100:3-5

I will sing of the mercies of the Lord for ever: with my mouth will I make known thy faithfulness to all generations.

For I have said, Mercy shall be built up for ever; thy faithfulness shalt thou establish in the very heavens.

I have made a covenant with my chosen, I have sworn unto David my servant,

Thy seed will I establish for ever and build up thy throne to all generations. Selah.

Psalms 89:1-4

This shall be written for the generation to come: and the people which shall be created shall praise the Lord.

Psalms 102:18

Sing and rejoice, O daughter of Zion: for, lo, I come, and I will dwell in the midst of thee, saith the Lord.

Zechariah 2:10

Nebuchadnezzar the king, unto all people, nations, and languages, that dwell in all the earth; Peace be multiplied unto you.

I thought it good to shew the signs and wonders that the high God hath wrought toward me.

How great are his signs! and how mighty are his wonders! his kingdom is an everlasting kingdom, and his dominion is from generation to generation.

Daniel 4:1-3

I thank thee, and praise thee, O thou God of my fathers, who hast given me wisdom and might, and hast made known unto me now what we desired of thee: for thou hast now made known unto us the king's matter.

Daniel 2:23

But ye are a chosen generation, a royal priesthood, an holy nation, a peculiar people; that ye should shew forth the praises of him who hath called you out of darkness into his marvellous light:

I Peter 2:9

The Lord shall increase you more and more, you and your children.

Ye are blessed of the Lord which made heaven and earth.

The heaven, even the heavens, are the Lord's: but the earth hath he given to the children of men.

The dead praise not the Lord, neither any that go down into silence.

But we will bless the Lord from this time forth and for evermore. Praise the Lord.

Psalms 115:14-18

Your children grow to love Him

I love them that love me; and those that seek me early shall find me.

Proverbs 8:17

And the child Samuel grew on, and was in favour both with the Lord, and also with men.

I Samuel 2:26

The Lord shall establish thee an holy people unto himself, as he hath sworn unto thee, if thou shalt keep the commandments of the Lord thy God, and walk in his ways.

And all people of the earth shall see that thou art called by the name of the Lord; and they shall be afraid of thee.

Deuteronomy 28:9, 10

Ye are the salt of the earth: but if the salt have lost his savour, wherewith shall it be salted? it is thenceforth good for nothing, but to be cast out, and to be trodden under foot of men.

Ye are the light of the world. A city that is set on an hill cannot be hid.

Neither do men light a candle, and put it under a bushel, but on a candlestick; and it giveth light unto all that are in the house.

Let your light so shine before men, that they may see your good works, and glorify your Father which is in heaven.

Matthew 5:13-16

That Christ may dwell in your hearts by faith; that ye, being rooted and grounded in love,

May be able to comprehend with all saints what is the breadth, and length, and depth, and height;

And to know the love of Christ, which passeth knowledge, that ye might be filled with all the fulness of God.

Ephesians 3:17-19

At the same time, saith the Lord, will I be the God of all the families of Israel, and they shall be my people.

The Lord hath appeared of old unto me, saying, Yea, I have loved thee with an everlasting love: therefore with loving kindness have I drawn thee.

Jeremiah 31:1, 3

...Knowledge puffeth up, but charity edifieth.

And if any man think that he knoweth any thing, he knoweth nothing yet as he ought to know.

But if any man love God, the same is known of him.

I Corinthians 8:1b-3

And thou shalt love the Lord thy God with all thy heart, and with all thy soul, and with all thy mind, and with all thy strength: this is the first commandment.

Mark 12:30

Grace be unto you, and peace, from God our Father, and from the Lord Jesus Christ.

I thank my God always on your behalf, for the grace of God which is given you by Jesus Christ;

That in every thing ye are enriched by him, in all utterance, and in all knowledge;

Even as the testimony of Christ was confirmed in you:

So that ye come behind in no gift; waiting for the coming of our Lord Jesus Christ:

Who shall also confirm you unto the end, that ye may be blameless in the day of our Lord Jesus Christ.

God is faithful, by whom ye were called unto the fellowship of his Son Jesus Christ our Lord.

I Corinthians 1:3-9

Your family worships together

And when we cried unto the Lord God of our fathers, the Lord heard our voice, and looked on our affliction, and our labour, and our oppression:

And now, behold, I have brought the first-fruits of the land, which thou, O Lord, hast given me. And thou shalt set it before the Lord thy God, and worship before the Lord thy God:

Deuteronomy 26:7, 10

O come, let us worship and bow down: let us kneel before the Lord our maker.

For he is our God; and we are the people of his pasture, and the sheep of his hand. . . .

Psalms 95:6, 7

I will also praise thee with the psaltery, even thy truth, O my God: unto thee will I sing with the harp, O thou Holy One of Israel.

My lips shall greatly rejoice when I sing unto thee; and my soul, which thou hast redeemed.

My tongue also shall talk of thy righteousness all the day long: for they are confounded, for they are brought unto shame, that seek my hurt.

Psalms 71:22-24

The Lord liveth; and blessed be my rock; and exalted be the God of the rock of my salvation.

II Samuel 22:47

Exalt the Lord our God, and worship at his holy hill; for the Lord our God is holy.

Make a joyful noise unto the Lord, all ye lands.

Serve the Lord with gladness come before his presence with singing.

Psalms 99:9, 100:1-2

Let them give glory unto the Lord, and declare his praise in the islands.

Isaiah 42:12

To whom then will ye liken God? or what likeness will ye compare unto him?

Have ye not known? have ye not heard? hath it not been told you from the beginning? have ye not understood from the foundations of the earth?

It is he that sitteth upon the circle of the earth, and the inhabitants thereof are as grasshoppers; that stretcheth out the heavens as a curtain, and spreadeth them out as a tent to dwell in:

Isaiah 40:18, 21, 22

This people have I formed for myself; they shall shew forth my praise.

Isaiah 43:21

Therefore my people shall know my name: therefore they shall know in that day that I am he that doth speak: behold, it is I.

Isaiah 52:6

Then shalt thou delight thyself in the Lord; and I will cause thee to ride upon the high places of the earth, and feed thee with the heritage of Jacob thy father: for the mouth of the Lord hath spoken it.

Isaiah 58:14

Jesus saith unto her, Woman, believe me, the hour cometh, when ye shall neither in this mountain, nor yet at Jerusalem, worship the Father.

Ye worship ye know not what: we know what we worship: for salvation is of the Jews.

But the hour cometh, and now is, when the true worshippers shall worship the Father in spirit and in truth: for the Father seeketh such to worship him.

God is a Spirit: and they that worship him must worship him in spirit and in truth.

John 4:21-24

Then saith Jesus unto him, Get thee hence, Satan: for it is written, Thou shalt worship the Lord thy God, and him only shalt thou serve.

Matthew 4:10

Then Paul stood in the midst of Mars' hill, and said, Ye men of Athens, I perceive that in all things ye are too superstitious.

For as I passed by, and beheld your devotions, I found an altar with this inscription, TO THE UNKNOWN GOD. Whom therefore ye ignorantly worship, him declare I unto you.

For in him we live, and move, and have our being; as certain also of your own poets have said, For we are also his offspring.

Forasmuch then as we are the offspring of God, we ought not to think that the Godhead is like unto gold, or silver, or stone, graven by art and man's device.

And the times of this ignorance God winked at; but now commandeth all men every where to repent:

Acts 17:22, 23, 28-30

Let the word of Christ dwell in you richly in all wisdom; teaching and admonishing one another in psalms and hymns and spiritual songs, singing with grace in your hearts to the Lord.

Colossians 3:16

God Keeps You Secure When...

Your family faces its enemies

The eternal God is thy refuge, and underneath are the everlasting arms: and he shall thrust out the enemy from before thee; and shall say, Destroy them.

Deuteronomy 33:27

Be strong and of a good courage, fear not, nor be afraid of them: for the Lord thy God, he it is that doth go with thee; he will not fail thee, nor forsake thee.

Deuteronomy 31:6

But if thou shalt indeed obey his voice, and do all that I speak; then I will be an enemy unto thine enemies, and an adversary unto thine adversaries.

Exodus 23:22

Arise, O Lord; O God, lift up thine hand: forget not the humble.

Wherefore doth the wicked contemn God? he hath said in his heart, Thou wilt not require it.

Thou hast seen it; for thou beholdest mischief and spite, to requite it with thy hand: the poor committeth himself unto thee; thou art the helper of the fatherless.

Break thou the arm of the wicked and the evil man: seek out his wickedness till thou find none.

The Lord is King for ever and ever: the heathen are perished out of his land.

Lord, thou hast heard the desire of the humble: thou wilt prepare their heart, thou wilt cause thine ear to hear:

To judge the fatherless and the oppressed, that the man of the earth may no more oppress.

Psalms 10:12-18

He suffered no man to do them wrong: yea, he reproved kings for their sakes;

Saying, Touch not mine anointed, and do my prophets no harm.

Psalms 105:14, 15

Then the king arose very early in the morning, and went in haste unto the den of lions.

And when he came to the den, he cried with a lamentable voice unto Daniel: and the king spake and said to Daniel, O Daniel, servant of the living God, is thy God, whom thou servest continually, able to deliver thee from the lions?

Then said Daniel unto the king, O king, live for ever.

My God hath sent his angel, and hath shut the lions' mouths, that they have not hurt me: forasmuch as before him innocency was found in me; and also before thee, O king, have I done no hurt.

Daniel 6:19-22

Keep not thou silence, O God: hold not thy peace, and be not still, O God.

For, lo, thine enemies make a tumult: and they that hate thee have lifted up the head.

They have taken crafty counsel against thy people, and consulted against thy hidden ones.

Psalms 83:1-3

Shadrach, Meshach, and Abednego, answered and said to the king, O Nebuchadnezzar, we are not careful to answer thee in this matter.

If it be so, our God whom we serve is able to deliver us from the burning fiery furnace, and he will deliver us out of thine hand, O king.

But if not, be it known unto thee, O king, that we will not serve thy gods, nor worship the golden image which thou hast setup.

Then was Nebuchadnezzar full of fury, and the form of his visage was changed against Shadrach, Meshach, and Abednego: therefore he spake, and commanded that they should heat the furnace one seven times more than it was wont to be heated.

And these three men, Shadrach, Meshach, and Abednego, fell down bound into the mist of the burning fiery furnace.

Then Nebuchadnezzar the king was astonied, and rose up in haste, and spake, and said unto his counsellors, Did not we cast three men bound into the midst of the fire? They answered and said unto the king, True, O king.

He answered and said, Lo, I see four men loose, walking in the midst of the fire, and they have no hurt; and the form of the fourth is like the Son of God.

Daniel 3:16-19, 23-25

Submit yourselves therefore to God. Resist the devil, and he will flee from you.

James 4:7

I will love thee, O Lord, my strength.

The Lord is my rock, and my fortress, and my deliverer; my God, my strength, in whom I will trust; my buckler, and the horn of my salvation, and my high tower.

I will call upon the Lord, who is worthy to be praised: so shall I be saved from mine enemies.

Psalms 18:1-3

You need to make a major job change

Labour not to be rich: cease from thine own wisdom.

Wilt thou set thine eyes upon that which is not? for riches certainly make themselves wings; they fly away as an eagle toward heaven.

Proverbs 23:4, 5

Put not your trust in princes, nor in the son of man, in whom there is no help.

His breath goeth forth, he returneth to his earth; in that very day his thoughts perish.

Happy is he that hath the God of Jacob for his help, whose hope is in the Lord his God:

Psalms 146:3-5

Again, I considered all travail, and every right work, that for this a man is envied of his neighbour. This is also vanity and vexation of spirit.

The fool foldeth his hands together, and eateth his own flesh.

Better is an handful with quietness, than both the hands full with travail and vexation of spirit.

Ecclesiastes 4:4-6

For the scripture saith, Thou shalt not muzzle the ox that treadeth out the corn. And, The labourer is worthy of his reward.

I Timothy 5:18

What profit hath he that worketh in that wherein he laboureth?

I have seen the travail, which God hath given to the sons of men to be exercised in it.

He hath made every thing beautiful in his time: also he hath set the world in their heart, so that no man can find out the work that God maketh from the beginning to the end.

I know that there is no good in them, but for a man to rejoice, and to do good in his life.

And also that every man should eat and drink, and enjoy the good of all his labour, it is the gift of God.

Ecclesiastes 3:9-13

Yea, I hated all my labour which I had taken under the sun: because I should leave it unto the man that shall be after me.

And who knoweth whether he shall be a wise man or a fool? yet shall he have rule over all my labour wherein I have laboured, and wherein I have shewed myself wise under the sun. This is also vanity.

Therefore I went about to cause my heart to despair of all the labour which I took under the sun.

For God giveth to a man that is good in his sight wisdom, and knowledge, and joy: but to the sinner he giveth travail, to gather and to heap up, that he may give to him that is good before God. This also is vanity and vexation of spirit.

Ecclesiastes 2:18-20, 26

The name of the Lord is a strong tower: the righteous runneth into it, and is safe.

Proverbs 18:10

Therefore I say unto you, Take no thought for your life, what ye shall eat, or what ye shall drink; nor yet for your body, what ye shall put on. Is not the life more than meat, and the body than raiment?

Behold the fowls of the air: for they sow not, neither do they reap, nor gather into barns; yet your heavenly Father feedeth them. Are ye not much better than they?

Which of you by taking thought can add one cubit unto his stature?

And why take ye thought for raiment? Consider the lilies of the field, how they grow; they toil not, neither do they spin:

And yet I say unto you, That even Solomon in all his glory was not arrayed like one of these.

Wherefore, if God so clothe the grass of the field, which to day is, and to morrow is cast into the oven, shall he not much more clothe you, O ye of little faith?

Therefore take no thought, saying, What shall we eat, or, What shall we drink? or, Wherewithal shall we be clothed?

(For after all these things do the Gentiles seek:) for your heavenly Father knoweth that ye have need of all these things.

But seek ye first the kingdom of God, and his righteousness; and all these things shall be added unto you.

Take therefore no thought for the morrow: for the morrow shall take thought for the things of itself. Sufficient unto the day is the evil thereof.

Matthew 6:25-34

For other foundation can no man lay than that is laid, which is Jesus Christ.

Now if any man build upon this foundation gold, silver, precious stones, wood, hay, stubble;

Every man's work shall be made manifest: for the day shall declare it, because it shall be revealed by fire; and the fire shall try every man's work of what sort it is.

If any man's work abide which he hath built thereupon, he shall receive a reward.

If any man's work shall be burned, he shall suffer loss: but he himself shall be saved; yet so as by fire.

I Corinthians 3:11-15

You worry about your family's health and well-being

For I will pour water upon him that is thirsty, and floods upon the dry ground: I will pour my spirit upon thy seed, and my blessing upon thine offspring:

Isaiah 44:3

The father of the righteous shall greatly rejoice: and he that begetteth a wise child shall have joy of him.

Thy father and thy mother shall be glad, and she that bare thee shall rejoice.

My son, give me thine heart, and let thine eyes observe my ways.

Proverbs 23:24-26

Thou wilt keep him in perfect peace, whose mind is stayed on thee: because he trusteth in thee.

Isaiah 26:3

The eyes of all wait upon thee; and thou givest them their meat in due season.

Thou openest thine hand, and satisfiest the desire of every living thing.

The Lord is righteous in all his ways, and holy in all his works.

The Lord is nigh unto all them that call upon him, to all that call upon him in truth.

He will fulfil the desire of them that fear him: he also will hear their cry, and will save them.

The Lord preserveth all them that love him: but all the wicked will he destroy.

My mouth shall speak the praise of the Lord: and let all flesh bless his holy name for ever and ever.

Psalms 145:15-21

And the work of righteousness shall be peace; and the effect of righteousness quietness and assurance for ever.

Isaiah 32:17

And, behold, Boaz came from Bethlehem, and said unto the reapers, The Lord be with you. And they answered him, The Lord bless thee.

Then said Boaz unto his servant that was set over the reapers, Whose damsel is this?

And the servant that was set over the reapers answered and said, It is the Moabitish damsel that came back with Naomi out of the country of Moab:

And she said, I pray you, let me glean and gather after the reapers among the sheaves: so she came, and hath continued even from the morning until now, that she tarried a little in the house.

Then said Boaz unto Ruth, Hearest thou not, my daughter? Go not to glean in another field, neither go from hence, but abide here fast by my maidens:

Let thine eyes be on the field that they do reap, and go thou after them: have I not charged the young men that they shall not touch thee? and when thou art athirst, go unto the vessels, and drink of that which the young men have drawn.

Then she fell on her face, and bowed herself to the ground, and said unto him, Why have I found grace in thine eyes, that thou shouldest take knowledge of me, seeing I am a stranger?

And Boaz answered and said unto her, It hath fully been shewed me, all that thou hast done unto thy mother in law since the death of thine husband: and how thou hast left thy father and thy mother, and the land of thy nativity, and art come unto a people which thou knewest not heretofore.

The Lord recompense thy work, and a full reward be given thee of the Lord God of Israel, under whose wings thou art come to trust.

Ruth 2:4-12

Blessed is every one that feareth the Lord; that walketh in his ways.

For thou shalt eat the labour of thine hands: happy shalt thou be, and it shall be well with thee.

Thy wife shall be as a fruitfull vine by the sides of thine house: thy children like olive plants round about thy table.

Behold, that thus shall the man be blessed that feareth the Lord.

The Lord shall bless thee out of Zion: and thou shalt see the good of Jerusalem all the days of thy life.

Yea, thou shalt see thy children's children, and peace upon Israel.

Psalms 128:1-6

But because the Lord loved you, and because he would keep the oath which he had sworn unto your fathers, hath the Lord brought you out with a mighty hand, and redeemed you out of the house of bondmen, from the hand of Pharaoh king of Egypt.

Know therefore that the Lord thy God, he is God, the faithful God, which keepeth covenant and mercy with them that love him and keep his commandments to a thousand generations;

Deuteronomy 7:8, 9

I will both lay me down in peace, and sleep: for thou, Lord, only makest me dwell in safety.

Psalms 4:8

Thy mercy, O Lord, is in the heavens; and thy faithfulness reacheth unto the clouds.

Psalms 36:5

Blessed be the Lord, who daily loadeth us with benefits, even the God of our salvation. Selah.

Psalms 68:19

Your child has trouble succeeding in school

Now I say, That the heir, as long as he is a child, differeth nothing from a servant, though he be lord of all;

But is under tutors and governors until the time appointed of the father.

Galatians 4:1, 2

Let no man deceive himself. If any man among you seemeth to be wise in this world, let him become a fool, that he may be wise.

For the wisdom of this world is foolishness with God. For it is written, He taketh the wise in their own craftiness.

I Corinthians 3:18, 19

For ye see your calling, brethren, how that not many wise men after the flesh, not many mighty, not many noble, are called:

But God hath chosen the foolish things of the world to confound the wise; and God hath chosen the weak things of the world to confound the things which are mighty;

And base things of the world, and things which are despised, hath God chosen, yea, and things which are not, to bring to nought things that are:

That no flesh should glory in his presence.

I Corinthains 1:26-29

And further, by these, my son, be admonished: of making many books there is no end; and much study is a weariness of the flesh.

Ecclesiastes 12:12

For if a man think himself to be something, when he is nothing, he deceiveth himself.

But let every man prove his own work, and then shall he have rejoicing in himself alone, and not in another.

For every man shall bear his own burden.

Let him that is taught in the word communicate unto him that teacheth in all good things.

Be not deceived; God is not mocked: for whatsoever a man soweth, that shall he also reap.

Galatians 6:3-7

And the king spake unto Ashpenaz the master of his eunuchs, that he should bring certain of the children of Israel, and of the king's seed, and of the princes;

Children in whom was no blemish, but well favoured, and skillful in all wisdom, and cunning in knowledge, and understanding science, and such as had ability in them to stand in the king's palace, and whom they might teach the learning and the tongue of the Chaldeans.

And the king appointed them a daily provision of the king's meat, and of the wine which he drank: so nourishing them three years, that at the end thereof they might stand before the king.

Now among these were of the children of Judah, Daniel, Hananiah, Mishael, and Azariah:

As for these four children, God gave them knowledge and skill in all learning and wisdom:

Daniel 1:3-6, 17a

Then was the secret revealed unto Daniel in a night vision. Then Daniel blessed the God of heaven.

Daniel answered and said, Blessed be the name of God for ever and ever: for wisdom and might are his:

And he changeth the times and the seasons: he removeth kings, and setteth up kings: he giveth wisdom unto the wise, and knowledge to them that know understanding:

He revealeth the deep and secret things: he knoweth what is in the darkness, and the light dwelleth with him.

I thank thee, and praise thee, O thou God of my fathers, who hast given me wisdom and might, and hast made known unto me now what we desired of thee: for thou hast now made known unto us the king's matter.

Daniel 2:19-23

For as we have many members in one body, and all members have not the same office:

So we, being many, are one body in Christ, and every one members one of another.

Having then gifts differing according to the grace that is given to us,

Romans 12:4-6a

Know ye not that they which run in a race run all, but one receiveth the prize? So run, that ye may obtain.

And every man that striveth for the mastery is temperate in all things. Now they do it to obtain a corruptible crown; but we an incorruptible.

I therefore so run, not as uncertainly; so fight I, not as one that beateth the air:

But I keep under my body, and bring it into subjection: lest that by any means, when I have preached to others, I myself should be a castaway.

I Corinthians 9:24-27

You don't have the money to pay the bills

I have been young, and now am old; yet have I not seen the righteous forsaken, nor his seed begging bread.

He is ever merciful, and lendeth; and his seed is blessed.

Depart from evil, and do good; and dwell for evermore.

For the Lord loveth judgment, and forsaketh not his saints; they are preserved for ever: but the seed of the wicked shall be cut off.

Psalms 37:25-28

The young lions do lack, and suffer hunger: but they that seek the Lord shall not want any good thing.

Psalms 34:10

The humble shall see this, and be glad: and your heart shall live that seek God.

For the Lord heareth the poor, and despiseth not his prisoners.

Let the heaven and earth praise him, the seas, and every thing that moveth therein.

Psalms 69:32-34

The Lord shall command the blessing upon thee in thy storehouses, and in all that thou settest thine hand unto; and he shall bless thee in the land which the Lord thy God giveth thee.

Deuteronomy 28:8

Wealth and riches shall be in his house: and his righteousness endureth for ever.

Psalms 112:3

The Lord is my shepherd;I shall not want.

Psalms 23:1

Ho, every one that thirsteth, come ye to the waters, and he that hath no money; come ye, buy, and eat; yea, come, buy wine and milk without money and without price.

Wherefore do ye spend money for that which is not bread? and your labour for that which safisfieth not? hearken diligently unto me, and eat ye that which is good, and let your soul delight itself in fatness.

Incline your ear, and come unto me: hear, and your soul shall live; and I will make an everlasting covenant with you, even the sure mercies of David.

Isaiah 55:1-3

When the poor and needy seek water, and there is none, and their tongue faileth for thirst, I the Lord will hear them, I the God of Israel will not forsake them.

Isaiah 41:17

And I will satiate the soul of the priests with fatness, and my people shall be satisfied with my goodness, saith the Lord.

Jeremiah 31:14

And ye shall eat in plenty, and be satisfied, and praise the name of the Lord your God, that hath dealt wondrously with you: and my people shall never be ashamed.

Joel 2:26

But my God shall supply all your need according to his riches in glory by Christ Jesus.

Philippians 4:19

God Comforts You When...

You feel inadequate in rearing your children

For the Lord God will help me; therfore shall I not be confounded; therefore have I set my face like a flint, and I know that I shall not be ashamed.

Isaiah 50:7

But thou art the same, and thy years shall have no end.

The children of thy servants shall continue, and their seed shall be established before thee.

Psalms 102:27, 28

For the eyes of the Lord run to and fro throughout the whole earth, to shew himself strong in the behalf of them whose heart is perfect toward him.

II Chronicles 16:9a

Lord, my heart is not haughty, nor mine eyes lofty: neither do I exercise myself in great matters, or in things too high for me.

Surely I have behaved and quieted myself, as a child that is weaned of his mother: my soul is even as a weaned child.

Let Israel hope in the Lord from henceforth and for ever.

Psalms 131:1-3

For who maketh thee to differ from another? and what hast thou that thou didst not receive? now if thou didst receive it, why dost thou glory, as if thou hadst not received it?

I Corinthians 4:7

But by the grace of God I am what I am: and his grace which was bestowed upon me was not in vain; but I laboured more abundantly than they all: yet not I, but the grace of God which was with me.

I Corinthians 15:10

Not that we are sufficient of ourselves to think any thing as of ourselves; but our sufficiency is of God;

II Corinthians 3:5

Knowest thou the time when the wild goats of the rock bring forth? or canst thou mark when the hinds do calve?

Canst thou number the months that they fulfil? or knowest thou the time when they bring forth?

They bow themselves, they bring forth their young ones, they cast out their sorrows.

Job 39:1-3

Gavest thou the goodly wings unto the peacocks? or wings and feathers unto the ostrich?

Which leaveth her eggs in the earth, and warmeth them in dust,

And forgetteth that the foot may crush them, or that the wild beast may break them.

She is hardened against her young ones, as though they were not hers: her labour is in vain without fear;

Because God hath deprived her of wisdom, neither hath he imparted to her understanding.

Job 39:13-17

Whereby are given unto us exceeding great and precious promises: that by these ye might be partakers of the divine nature, having escaped the corruption that is in the world through lust.

And beside this, giving all diligence, add to your faith virtue; and to virtue knowledge;

And to knowledge temperance; and to temperance patience; and to patience godliness;

And to godliness brotherly kindness; and to brotherly kindness charity.

For if these things be in you, and abound, they make you that ye shall neither be barren nor unfruitful in the knowledge of our Lord Jesus Christ.

II Peter 1:4-8

I have blotted out, as a thick cloud, thy transgressions, and, as a cloud, thy sins: return unto me; for I have redeemed thee.

Isaiah 44:22

But we were gentle among you, even as a nurse cherisheth her children:

So being affectionately desirous of you, we were willing to have imparted unto you, not the gospel of God only, but also our own souls, because ye were dear unto us.

I Thessalonians 2:7, 8

I can do all things through Christ which strengtheneth me.

Philippians 4:13

Come unto me, all ye that labour and are heavy laden, and I will give you rest.

Take my yoke upon you, and learn of me; for I am meek and lowly in heart: and ye shall find rest unto your souls.

For my yoke is easy, and my burden is light.

Matthew 11:28-30

Your child is seriously ill

Beloved, I wish above all things that thou mayest prosper and be in health, even as thy soul prospereth.

III John 2

And one of the multitude answered and said, Master, I have brought unto thee my son, which hath a dumb spirit;

And wheresoever he taketh him, he teareth him: and he foameth, and gnasheth with his teeth, and pineth away: and I spake to thy disciples that they should cast him out; and they could not.

He answereth him, and saith, O faithless generation, how long shall I be with you? how long shall I suffer you? bring him unto me.

And they brought him unto him: and when he saw him, straightway the spirit tare him; and he fell on the ground, and wallowed foaming.

And he asked his father, How long is it ago since this came unto him? And he said, Of a child.

And oftimes it hath cast him into the fire, and into the waters, to destroy him: but if thou canst do any thing; have compassion on us, and help us.

Jesus said unto him, If thou canst believe, all things are possible to him that believeth.

And straightway the father of the child cried out, and said with tears, Lord, I believe; help thou mine unbelief.

Mark 9:17-24

While he spake these things unto them, behold, there came a certain ruler, and worshipped him, saying, My daughter is even now dead: but come and lay thy hand upon her, and she shall live.

And Jesus arose, and followed him, and so did his disciples.

And when Jesus came into the ruler's house, and saw the minstrels and the people making a noise,

He said unto them, Give place: for the maid is not dead, but sleepeth. And they laughed him to scorn.

But when the people were put forth, he went in, and took her by the hand, and the maid arose.

And the fame hereof went abroad into all that land.

Matthew 9:18, 19, 23-26

And when Jesus was entered into Capernaum, there came unto him a centurion, beseeching him,

And saying, Lord, my servant lieth at home sick of the palsy, grievously tormented.

And Jesus saith unto him, I will come and heal him.

The centurion answered and said, Lord, I am not worthy that thou shouldest come under my roof: but speak the word only, and my servant shall be healed.

For I am a man under authority, having soldiers under me: and I say to this man, Go, and he goeth; and to another, Come, and he cometh; and to my servant, Do this, and he doeth it.

When Jesus heard it, he marvelled, and said to them that followed, Verily I say unto you, I have not found so great faith, no, not in Israel.

And I say unto you, That many shall come from the east and west, and shall sit down with Abraham, and Isaac, and Jacob, in the kingdom of heaven.

But the children of the kingdom shall be cast out into outer darkness: there shall be weeping and gnashing of teeth.

And Jesus said unto the centurion, Go thy way; and as thou hast believed, so be it done unto thee. And his servant was healed in the selfsame hour.

Matthew 8:5-13

And Nathan departed unto his house. And the Lord struck the child that Uriah's wife bare unto David, and it was very sick.

David therefore besought God for the child; and David fasted, and went in, and lay all night upon the earth.

And the elders of his house arose, and went to him, to raise him up from the earth: but he would not, neither did he eat bread with them.

And it came to pass on the seventh day, that the child died. And the servants of David feared to tell him that the child was dead: for they said, Behold, while the child was yet alive, we spake unto him, and he would not hearken unto our voice: how will he then vex himself, if we tell him that the child is dead?

But when David saw that his servants whispered, David perceived that the child was dead: therefore David said unto his servants, Is the child dead? And they said, He is dead.

Then David arose from the earth, and washed, and anointed himself, and changed his apparel, and came into the house of the Lord, and worshipped: then he came to his own house; and when he required, they set bread before him, and he did eat.

Then said his servants unto him, What thing is this that thou hast done? thou didst fast and weep for the child, while it was alive; but when the child was dead, thou didst rise and eat bread.

And he said, While the child was yet alive, I fasted and wept: for I said, Who can tell whether God will be gracious to me, that the child may live?

But now he is dead, wherefore should I fast? can I bring him back again? I shall go to him, but he shall not return to me.

And David comforted Bathsheba his wife, and went in unto her, and lay with her: and she bare a son, and he called his name Solomon: and the Lord loved him.

II Samuel 12:15-24

Is any sick among you? let him call for the elders of the church; and let them pray over him, anointing him with oil in the name of the Lord:

And the prayer of faith shall save the sick, and the Lord shall raise him up; and if he have committed sins, they shall be forgiven him.

Confess your faults one to another, and pray one for another, that ye may be healed. The effectual fervent prayer of a righteous man availeth much.

James 5:14-16

As one whom his mother comforteth, so will I comfort you; and ye shall be comforted in Jerusalem.

Isaiah 66:13

Your wife doesn't seem to understand you

And the Lord God said, It is not good that the man should be alone; I will make him an help meet for him.

And Adam gave names to all cattle, and to the fowl of the air, and to every beast of the field; but for Adam there was not found an help meet for him.

And the Lord God caused a deep sleep to fall upon Adam, and he slept: and he took one of his ribs, and closed up the flesh instead thereof;

And the rib, which the Lord God had taken from man, made he a woman, and brought her unto the man.

And Adam said, This is now bone of my bones, and flesh of my flesh: she shall be called Woman, because she was taken out of Man.

Therefore shall a man leave his father and his mother, and shall cleave unto his wife: and they shall be one flesh.

And they were both naked, the man and his wife, and were not ashamed.

Genesis 2:18, 20-25

Likewise, ye husbands, dwell with them according to knowledge, giving honour unto the wife, as unto the weaker vessel, and as being heirs together of the grace of life; that your prayers be not hindered.

Finally, be ye all of one mind, having compassion one of another, love as brethren, be pitiful, be courteous:

Not rendering evil for evil, or railing for railing: but contrariwise blessing; knowing that ye are thereunto called, that ye should inherit a blessing.

For he that will love life, and see good days, let him refrain his tongue from evil, and his lips that they speak no guile:

Let hem eschew evil, and do good; let him seek peace, and ensue it.

I Peter 3:7-11

A word fitly spoken is like apples of gold in pictures of silver.

By long forbearing is a prince persuaded, and a soft tongue breaketh the bone.

Proverbs 25:11, 15

Though I speak with the tongues of men and of angels, and have not charity, I am become as sounding brass, or a tinkling cymbal.

And though I have the gift of prophecy, and understand all mysteries, and all knowledge; and though I have all faith, so that I could remove mountains, and have not charity, I am nothing.

And though I bestow all my goods to feed the poor, and though I give my body to be burned, and have not charity, it profiteth me nothing.

Charity suffereth long, and is kind; charity envieth not; charity vaunteth not itself, is not puffed up,

Doth not behave itself unseemly, seeketh not her own, is not easily provoked, thinketh no evil;

Rejoiceth not in iniquity, but rejoiceth in the truth;

Beareth all things, believeth all things, hopeth all things, endureth all things.

Charity never faileth: but whether there be prophesies, they shall fail; whether there be tongues, they shall cease; whether there be knowledge, it shall vanish away.

For we know in part, and we prophesy in part.

But when that which is perfect is come, then that which is in part shall be done away.

When I was a child I spake as a child, I understood as a child, I thought as a child: but when I became a man, I put away childish things.

For now we see through a glass, darkly; but then face to face: now know in part; but then shall I know even as also I am known.

And now abideth faith, hope, charity, these three; but the greatest of these is charity.

I Corinthians 13:1-13

Let love be without dissimulation. Abhor that which is evil; cleave to that which is good.

Be kindly affectioned one to another with brotherly love; in honour preferring one another;
Romans 12:9, 10

Owe no man any thing, but to love one another: for he that loveth another hath fulfilled the law.

For this, Thou shalt not commit adultery, Thou shalt not kill, Thou shalt not steal, Thou shalt not bear false witness, Thou shalt not covet; and if there be any other commandment, it is briefly comprehended in this saying, namely, Thou shalt love thy neighbour as thyself.

Love worketh no ill to his neighbour: therefore love is the fulfilling of the law.

Romans 13:8-10

Nevertheless neither is the man without the woman, neither the woman without the man, in the Lord.

For as the woman is of the man, even so is the man also by the woman; but all things of God.

I Corinthians 11:11, 12

For none of us liveth to himself, and no man dieth to himself.

Romans 14:7

As a bird that wandereth from her nest, so is a man that wandereth from his place.

Proverbs 27:8

Two are better than one; because they have a good reward for their labour.

For if they fall, the one will lift up his fellow: but woe to him that is alone when he falleth; for he hath not another to help him up.

Again, if two lie together, then they have heat: but how can one be warm alone?

Ecclesiastes 4:9-11

For if ye love them which love you, what reward have ye? do not even the publicans the same?

And if ye salute your brethren only, what do ye more than others? do not even the publicans so?

Be ye therefore perfect, even as your Father which is in heaven is perfect.

Matthew 5:46-48

You must discipline your children

My son, despise not the chastening of the Lord; neither be weary of his correction:

For whom the Lord loveth he correcteth; even as a father the son in whom he delighteth.

Proverbs 3:11, 12

Furthermore we have had fathers of our flesh which corrected us, and we gave them reverence: shall we not much rather be in subjection unto the Father of spirits, and live?

For they verily for a few days chastened us after their own pleasure; but he for our profit, that we might be partakers of his holiness.

Now no chastening for the present seemeth to be joyous, but grievous: neverthless afterward it yieldeth the peaceable fruit of righteousness unto them which are exercised thereby.

Hebrews 12:9-11

The rod and reproof give wisdom: but a child left to himself bringeth his mother to shame.

Correct thy son, and he shall give thee rest; yea, he shall give delight unto thy soul.

Proverbs 29:15, 17

Though he were a Son, yet learned he obedience by the things which he suffered;

Hebrews 5:8

Now I rejoice, not that ye were made sorry, but that ye sorrowed to repentance: for ye were made sorry after a godly manner, that ye might receive damage by us in nothing.

II Corinthians 7:9

Thou shalt beat him with the rod, and shalt deliver his soul from hell.

Proverbs 23:14

Chasten thy son while there is hope, and let not thy soul spare for his crying.

Proverbs 19:18

A reproof entereth more into a wise man that an hundred stripes into a fool.

Proverbs 17:10

Hatred stirreth up strifes: but love covereth all sins.

In the lips of him that hath understanding wisdom is found: but a rod is for the back of him that is void of understanding.

Proverbs 10:12, 13

Whoso loveth instruction loveth knowledge: but he that hateth reproof is brutish.

A good man obtaineth favour of the Lord: but a man of wicked devices will he condemn.

A man shall not be established by wickedness: but the root of the righteous shall not be moved.

Proverbs 12:1-3

Sanctify yourselves therefore and be ye holy: for I am the Lord your God.

Leviticus 20:7

Be ye therefore very courageous to keep and to do all that is written in the book of the law of Moses, that ye turn not aside therefrom to the right hand or to the left;

But cleave unto the Lord your God, as ye have done unto this day.

Joshua 23:6, 8

My son, keep my words, and lay up my commandments with thee.

Keep my commandments, and live; and my law as the apple of thine eye.

Bind them upon thy fingers, write them upon the table of thine heart.

Proverbs 7:1-3

You feel powerless to shield your children from evils like drugs and alcohol

Hear, O heavens, and give ear, O earth: for the Lord hath spoken, I have nourished and brought up children, and they have rebelled against me.

Isaiah 1:2

In the fear of the Lord is strong confidence: and his children shall have a place of refuge.

The fear of the Lord is a fountain of life, to depart from the snares of death.

Proverbs 14:26, 27

Hear me now therefore, O ye children, and depart not from the words of my mouth.

Lest strangers be filled with thy wealth; and thy labours be in the house of a stranger;

And thou mourn at the last, when thy flesh and thy body are consumed,

And say, How have I hated instruction, and my heart despised reproof;

And have not obeyed the voice of my teachers, nor inclined mine ear to them that instructed me!

I was almost in all evil in the midst of the congregation and assembly.

Proverbs 5:7, 10-14

In the way of righteousness is life; and in the pathway thereof there is no death.

Proverbs 12:28

Wine is a mocker, strong drink is raging: and whosoever is deceived thereby is not wise.

Proverbs 20:1

A foolish son is a grief to his father, and bitterness to her that bare him.

Proverbs 17:25

He that loveth pleasure shall be a poor man: he that loveth wine and oil shall not be rich.

Proverbs 21:17

By mercy and truth iniquity is purged: and by the fear of the Lord men depart from evil.

Proverbs 16:6

Take away the dross from the silver, and there shall come forth a vessel for the finer.

Proverbs 25:4

Know ye not that ye are the temple of God, and that the Spirit of God dwelleth in you?

If any man defile the temple of God, him shall God destroy; for the temple of God is holy, which temple ye are.

I Corinthians 3:16, 17

My son, if sinners entice thee, consent thou not.

So are the ways of every one that is greedy of gain; which taketh away the life of the owners thereof.

Proverbs 1:10, 19

And fear not them which kill the body, but are not able to kill the soul: but rather fear him which is able to destroy both soul and body in hell.

Matthew 10:28

For the law of the Spirit of life in Christ Jesus hath made me free from the law of sin and death.

Romans 8:2

The merciful man doeth good to his own soul: but he that is cruel troubleth his own flesh.

Though hand join in hand, the wicked shall not be unpunished: but the seed of the righteous shall be delivered.

Proverbs 11:17, 21

But whoso hearkeneth unto me shall dwell safely, and shall be quiet from fear of evil.

Proverbs 1:33

My son, if thou wilt receive my words, and hide my commandments with thee;

So that thou incline thine ear unto wisdom, and apply thine heart to understanding;

Yea, if thou criest after knowledge, and liftest up thy voice for understanding;

If thou seekest her as silver, and searchest for her as for hid treasures;

Then shalt thou understand the fear of the Lord, and find the knowledge of God.

For the Lord giveth wisdom: out of his mouth cometh knowledge and understanding.

He layeth up sound wisdom for the righteous: he is a buckler to them that walk uprightly.

He keepeth the paths of judgment, and preserveth the way of his saints.

Then shalt thou understand righteousness, and judgment, and equity; yea, every good path.

Proverbs 2:1-9

God's Special Love Is With You When...

You bring your problems to Him

For the Lord will not forsake his people for his great name's sake: because it hath pleased the Lord to make you his people.

I Samuel 12:22

If thou prepare thine heart, and stretch out thine hands toward him;

If iniquity be in thine hand, put it far away, and let not wickedness dwell in thy tabernacles.

For then shalt thou lift up thy face without spot; yea, thou shalt be stedfast, and shalt not fear:

Because thou shalt forget thy misery, and remember it as waters that pass away:

And thine age shall be clearer than the noonday; thou shalt shine forth, thou shalt be as the morning.

And thou shalt be secure, because there is hope; yea, thou shalt dig about thee, and thou shalt take thy rest in safety.

Job 11:13-18

Blessed be the Lord, that hath given rest unto his people Israel, according to all that he promised: there hath not failed one word of all his good promise, which he promised by the hand of Moses his servant.

The Lord our God be with us, as he was with our fathers: let him not leave us, nor forsake us:

That he may incline our hearts unto him, to walk in all his ways, and to keep his commandments, and his statutes, and his judgments, which he commanded our fathers.

And let these my words, wherewith I have made supplication before the Lord, be nigh unto the Lord our God day and night, that he maintain the cause of his servant, and the cause of his people Israel at all times, as the matter shall require:

I Kings 8:56-59

For the eyes of the Lord are over the righteous, and his ears are open unto their prayers: but the face of the Lord is against them that do evil.

And who is he that will harm you, if ye be followers of that which is good?

But and if ye suffer for righteousness' sake, happy are ye: and be not afraid of their terror, neither be troubled;

But sanctify the Lord God in your hearts: and be ready always to give an answer to every man that asketh you a reason of the hope that is in you with meekness and fear:

I Peter 3:12-15

And to you who are troubled rest with us, when the Lord Jesus shall be revealed from heaven with his mighty angels,

In flaming fire taking vengeance on them that know not God, and that obey not the gospel of our Lord Jesus Christ:

Who shall be punished with everlasting destruction from the presence of the Lord, and from the glory of his power;

When he shall come to be glorified in his saints, and to be admired in all them that believe (because our testimony among you was believed) in that day.

Wherefore also we pray always for you, that our God would count you worthy of this calling, and fulfil all the good pleasure of his goodness, and the work of faith with power:

That the name of our Lord Jesus Christ may be glorified in you, and yet in him, according to the grace of our God and the Lord Jesus Christ.

II Thessalonians 1:7-12

But Jesus beheld them, and said unto them, With men this is impossible; but with God all things are possible.

Matthew 19:26

But we had the sentence of death in oursleves, that we should not trust in ourselves, but in God which raiseth the dead:

Who delivered us from so great a death, and doth deliver: in whom we trust that he will yet deliver us;

II Corinthians 1:9, 10

Consider what I say: and the Lord give thee understanding in all things.

It is a faithful saying: For if we be dead with him, we shall also live with him:

If we suffer, we shall also reign with him: if we deny him, he also will deny us:

II Timothy 2: 7, 11, 12

The Spirit of the Lord God is upon me; because the Lord hath anointed me to preach good tidings unto the meek; he hath sent me to bind up the brokenhearted, to proclaim liberty to the captives, and the opening of the prison to them that are bound;

To proclaim the acceptable year of the Lord, and the day of vengeance of our God; to comfort all that mourn;

To appoint unto them that mourn in Zion, to give unto them beauty for ashes, the oil of joy for mourning, the garment of praise for the spirit of heaviness; that they might be called trees of righteousness, the planting of the Lord, that he might be glorified.

Isaiah 61:1-3

We are troubled on every side, yet not distressed; we are perplexed, but not in despair;

Persecuted, but not forsaken; cast down, but not destroyed;

Always bearing about in the body the dying of the Lord Jesus, that the life also of Jesus might be made manifest in our body.

For all things are for your sakes, that the abundant grace might through the thanksgiving of many redound to the glory of God.

For which cause we faint not; but though our outward man perish, yet the inward man is renewed day by day.

For our light affliction, which is but for a moment, worketh for us a far more exceeding and eternal weight of glory;

While we look not at the things which are seen, but at the things which are not seen: for the things which are seen are temporal; but the things which are not seen are eternal.

II Corinthians 4:8-10, 15-18

Now thanks be unto God, which always causeth us to triumph in Christ, and maketh manifest the savour of his knowledge by us in every place.

For we are unto God a sweet savour of Christ, in them that are saved, and in them that perish:

To the one we are the savour of death unto death; and to the other the savour of life unto life. And who is sufficient for these things?

For we are not as many, which corrupt the word of God: but as of sincerity, but as of God, in the sight of God speak we in Christ.

II Corinthians 2:14-17

You rely on Him to guide and direct your children

My little children, these things write I unto you, that ye sin not. And if any man sin, we have an advocate with the Father, Jesus Christ the righteous:

I John 2:1

For the Son of man is come to seek and to save that which was lost.

Luke 19:10

Hast thou not known? hast thou not heard, that the everlasting God, the Lord, the Creator of the ends of the earth, fainteth not, neither is weary? there is no searching of his understanding.

He giveth power to the faint; and to them that have no might he increaseth strength.

Even the youths shall faint and be weary, and the young men shall utterly fall:

But they that wait upon the Lord shall renew their strength; they shall mount up with wings as eagles; they shall run, and not be weary; and they shall walk, and not faint.

Isaiah 40:28-31

He will keep the feet of his saints, and the wicked shall be silent in darkness; for by strength shall no man prevail.

I Samuel 2:9

I am a companion of all them that fear thee, and of them that keep thy precepts.

Psalms 119:63

When thou goest, it shall lead thee; when thou sleepest, it shall keep thee; and when thou awakest, it shall talk with thee.

For the commandment is a lamp; and the law is light; and reproofs of instruction are the way of life:

Proverbs 6:22, 23

I the Lord have called thee in righteousness, and will hold thine hand, and will keep thee, and give thee for a covenant of the people, for a light of the Gentiles;

Isaiah 42:6

I will go before thee, and make the crooked places straight: I will break in pieces the gates of brass, and cut in sunder the bars of iron:

And I will give thee the treasures of darkness, and hidden riches of secret places, that thou mayest know that I, the Lord, which call thee by thy name, am the God of Israel.

Isaiah 45:2, 3

Remember ye not the former things, neither consider the things of old.

Behold, I will do a new thing; now it shall spring forth; shall ye not know it? I will even make a way in the wilderness, and rivers in the desert.

Isaiah 43:18, 19

Fear thou not; for I am with thee: be not dismayed; for I am thy God: I willl strengthen thee; yea, I will help thee, yea, I will uphold thee with the right hand of my righteousness.

Isaiah 41:10

I have made the earth, and created man upon it: I, even my hands, have stretched out the heavens, and all their host have I commanded.

I have raised him up in righteousness, and I will direct all his ways: he shall build my city, and he shall let go my captives, not for price nor reward, saith the Lord of hosts.

Isaiah 45:12, 13

For the mountains shall depart, and the hills be removed; but my kindness shall not depart from thee, neither shall the covenant of my peace be removed, saith the Lord that hath mercy on thee.

Isaiah 54:10

For as the rain cometh down, and the snow from heaven, and returneth not thither, but watereth the earth, and maketh it bring forth and bud, that it may give seed to the sower, and bread to the eater:

So shall my word be that goeth forth out of my mouth: it shall not return unto me void, but it shall accomplish that which I please, and it shall prosper in the thing whereto I sent it.

Isaiah 55: 10:11

A man's heart deviseth his way: but the Lord directeth his steps.

Proverbs 16:9

(For we walk by faith, not by sight:)

II Corinthians 5:7

You forgive your children when they've done wrong

He made known his ways unto Moses, his acts unto the children of Israel.

The Lord is merciful and gracious, slow to anger, and plenteous in mercy.

He will not always chide: neither will he keep his anger for ever.

He hath not dealt with us after our sins; nor rewarded us according to our iniquities.

For as the heaven is high above the earth, so great is his mercy toward them that fear him.

As far as the east is from the west, so far hath he removed our transgressions from us.

Like as a father pitieth his children, so the Lord pitieth them that fear him.

Psalms 103:7 13

And he said, A certain man had two sons:

And the younger of them said to his father, Father, give me the portion of goods that falleth to me. And he divided unto them his living.

And not many days after the younger son gathered all together, and took his journey into a far country, and there wasted his substance with riotous living.

And when he had spent all, there arose a mighty famine in that land; and he began to be in want.

And he went and joined himself to a citizen of that country; and he sent him into his fields to feed swine.

And he would fain have filled his belly with the husks that the swine did eat: and no man gave unto him.

And when he came to himself, he said, How many hired servants of my father's have bread enough and to spare, and I perish with hunger!

I will arise and go to my father, and will say unto him, Father, I have sinned against heaven, and before thee,

And am no more worthy to be called thy son: make me as one of thy hired servants.

And he arose, and came to his father. But when he was yet a great way off, his father saw him, and had compassion, and ran, and fell on his neck, and kissed him.

And the son said unto him, Father, I have sinned against heaven, and in thy sight, and am no more worthy to be called thy son.

But the father said to his servants, Bring forth the best robe, and put it on him; and put a ring on his hand, and shoes on his feet:

And bring hither the fatted calf, and kill it; and let us eat, and be merry:

For this my son was dead, and is alive again; he was lost, and is found. And they began to be merry.

Luke 15:11-24

Then came Peter to him, and said, Lord, how oft shall my brother sin against me, and I forgive him? til seven times?

Jesus saith unto him, I say not unto thee,
Until seven times: but, Until seventy times seven.
Matthew 18:21, 22

You share your family's bounty with the poor

He that hath a bountiful eye shall be blessed; for he giveth of his bread to the poor.

Proverbs 22:9

Hearken, my beloved brethren, Hath not God chosen the poor of this world rich in faith, and heirs of the kingdom which he hath promised to them that love him?

James 2:5

Jesus said unto him, If thou wilt be perfect, go and sell that thou hast, and give to the poor, and thou shalt have treasure in heaven: and come and follow me.

But when the young man heard that saying, he went away sorrowful: for he had great possessions.

Then said Jesus unto his disciples, Verily I say unto you, That a rich man shall hardly enter in to the kingdom of heaven.

And again I say unto you, It is easier for a camel to go through the eye of a needle, than for a rich man to enter into the kingdom of God.

Matthew 19:21-24

What doth it profit, my brethren, though a man say he hath faith, and have not works? can faith save him?

If a brother or sister be naked, and destitute of daily food,

And one of you say unto them, Depart in peace, be ye warmed and filled; notwithstanding ye give them not those things which are needful to the body; what doth it profit?

Even so faith, if it hath not works, is dead, being alone.

James 2:14-17

Thou shalt surely give him, and thine heart shall not be grieved when thou givest unto him: because that for this thing the Lord thy God shall bless thee in all thy works, and in all that thou puttest thine hand unto.

For the poor shall never cease out of the land: therefore I command thee, saying, Thou shalt open thine hand wide unto thy brother, to thy poor, and to thy needy, in thy land.

Deuteronomy 15:10, 11

A poor man that oppresseth the poor is like a sweeping rain which leaveth no food.

Proverbs 28:3

He that oppresseth the poor reproacheth his Maker: but he that honoureth him hath mercy on the poor.

Proverbs 14:31

The Lord maketh poor, and maketh rich: he bringeth low, and lifteth up.

He raiseth up the poor out of the dust, and lifteth up the beggar from the dunghill, to set them among princes, and to make them inherit the throne of glory: for the pillars of the earth are the Lord's, and he hath set the world upon them.

I Samuel 2:7, 8

Whoso mocketh the poor reproacheth his Maker: and he that is glad at calamities shall not be unpunished.

Proverbs 17:5

And the multitude of them that believed were of one heart and of one soul: neither said any of them that aught of the things which he possessed was his own; but they had all things common.

And with great power gave the apostles witness of the ressurection of the Lord Jesus: and great grace was upon them all.

Neither was there any among them that lacked: for as many as were possessors of lands or houses sold them, and brought the prices of the things that were sold,

And laid them down at the apostles' feet: and distribution was made unto every man according as he had need.

Acts 4:32-35

Let the brother of low degree rejoice in that he is exalted:

But the rich, in that he is made low: because as the flower of the grass he shall pass away.

For the sun is no sooner risen with a burning heat, but it withereth the grass, and the flower thereof falleth, and the grace of the fashion of it perisheth: so also shall the rich man fade away in his ways.

James 1:9-11

He that hath a bountiful eye shall be blessed; for he giveth of his bread to the poor.

Proverbs 22:9

You bring your family together in prayer

For thus saith the Lord unto the eunuchs that keep my sabbaths, and choose the things that please me, and take hold of my covenant;

Even unto them will I give in mine house and within my walls a place and a name better than of sons and of daughters: I will give them an everlasting name, that shall not be cut off.

Also the sons of the stranger, that join themselves to the Lord, to serve him, and to love the name of the Lord, to be his servants, every one that keepeth the sabbath from polluting it, and taketh hold of my covenant;

Even them will I bring to my holy mountain, and make them joyful in my house of prayer: their burnt offerings and their sacrifices shall be accepted upon mine altar; for mine house shall be called an house of prayer for all people.

Isaiah 56:4-7

Delight thyself also in the Lord; and he shall give thee the desires of thine heart.

Psalms 37:4

And it shall come to pass, that before they call, I will answer; and while they are yet speaking, I will hear.

Isaiah 65:24

The Lord is nigh unto all them that call upon him, to all that call upon him in truth.

He will fulfil the desire of them that fear him: he also will hear their cry, and will save them.

Psalms 145:18, 19

And I set my face unto the Lord God, to seek by prayer and supplications, with fasting, and sackcloth, and ashes:

And I prayed unto the Lord my God, and made my confession, and said, O Lord, the great and dreadful God, keeping the covenant and mercy to them that love him, and to them that keep his commandments;

We have sinned, and have committed iniquity, and have done wickedly, and have rebelled, even by departing from thy precepts and from thy judgments:

Now therefore, O our God, hear the prayer of thy servant, and his supplications, and cause thy face to shine upon thy sanctuary that is desolate, for the Lord's sake.

O my God, incline thine ear, and hear; open thine eyes, and behold our desolations, and the city which is called by thy name: for we do not present our supplications before thee for our righteousnesses, but for thy great mercies.

Daniel 9:3-5, 17, 18

Call unto me, and I will answer thee, and shew thee great and mighty things, which thou knowest not.

Jeremiah 33:3

Ye also helping together by prayer for us, that for the gift bestowed upon us by the means of many persons thanks may be given by many on our behalf.

For our rejoicing is this, the testimony of our conscience, that in simplicity and godly sincerity, not with fleshly wisdom, but by the grace of God, we have had our conversation in the world, and more abundantly to you-ward.

For we write none other things unto you, than what ye read or acknowledge; and I trust ye shall acknowledge even to the end;

As also ye have acknowledged us in part, that we are your rejoicing, even as ye also are ours in the day of the Lord Jesus.

II Corinthians 1:11-14

And all things, whatsoever ye shall ask in prayer, believing, ye shall receive.

Matthew 21:22

Again I say unto you, That if two of you shall agree on earth as touching any thing that they shall ask, it shall be done for them of my Father which is in heaven.

For where two or three are gathered together in my name, there am I in the midst of them.

Matthew 18:19, 20

I will therefore that men pray every where, lifting up holy hands, without wrath and doubting.

I Timothy 2:8

Let us therefore come boldly unto the throne of grace, that we may obtain mercy, and find grace to help in time of need.

Hebrews 4:16

And whatsoever we ask, we receive of him, because we keep his commandments, and do those things that are pleasing in his sight.

I John 3:22

Rejoice in the Lord alway: and again I say, Rejoice.

Let your moderation be known unto all men. The Lord is at hand.

Be careful for nothing; but in every thing by prayer and supplication with thanksgiving let your requests be made known unto God.

And the peace of God, which passeth all understanding, shall keep your hearts and minds through Christ Jesus.

Philippians 4:4-7

God Shares Your Dreams For...

Children who know His love and share it with others

Be ye therefore followeres of God, as dear children;

And walk in love, as Christ also hath loved us, and hath given himself for us an offering and a sacrifice to God for a sweetsmelling savour.

Ephesians 5:1, 2

Now the end of the commandment is charity out of a pure heart, and of a good conscience, and of faith unfeigned:

I Timothy 1:5

And if ye call on the Father, who without respect of persons judgeth according to every man's work, pass the time of your sojourning here in fear:

Forasmuch as ye know that ye were not redeemed with corruptible things, as silver and gold, from your vain conversation received by tradition from your fathers;

But with the precious blood of Christ, as of a lamb without blemish and without spot:

Who verily was foreordained before the foundation of the world, but was manifest in these last times for you,

Who by him do believe in God that raised him up from the dead, and gave him glory; that your faith and hope might be in God.

Seeing ye have purified your souls in obeying the truth through the Spirit unto unfeigned love of the brethren, see that ye love one another with a pure heart fervently:

Being born again, not of corruptible seed, but of incorruptible, by the word of God, which liveth and abideth for ever.

I Peter 1:17-23

Again, a new commandment I write unto you, which thing is true in him and in you: because the darkness is past, and the true light now shineth.

He that saith he is in the light, and hateth his brother, is in darkness even until now.

He that loveth his brother abideth in the light, and there is none occasion of stumbling in him.

But he that hateth his brother is in darkness, and walketh in darkness, and knoweth not whither he goeth, because that darkness hath blinded his eyes.

I John 2:8-11

Now God himself and our Father, and our Lord Jesus Christ, direct our way unto you.

And the Lord make you to increase and abound in love one toward another, and toward all men, even as we do toward you:

I Thessalonians 3:11, 12

But as touching brotherly love ye need not that I write unto you: for ye yourselves are taught of God to love one another.

I Thessalonians 4:9

Put on therefore, as the elect of God, holy and beloved, bowels of mercies, kindness, humbleness of mind, meekness, longsuffering;

Forbearing one another, and forgiving one another, if any man have a quarrel against any: even as Christ forgave you, so also do ye.

And above all these things put on charity, which is the bond of perfectness.

Colossians 3:12-14

That Christ may dwell in your hearts by faith; that ye, being rooted and grounded in love,

May be able to comprehend with all saints what is the breadth, and length, and depth, and height;

And to know the love of Christ, which passeth knowledge, that ye might be filled with all the fulness of God.

Now unto him that is able to do exceeding abundantly above all that we ask or think, according to the power that worketh in us,

Unto him be glory in the church by Christ Jesus throughout all ages, world without end. Amen.

Ephesians 3:17-21

We give thanks to God and the Father of our Lord Jesus Christ, praying always for you,

Since we heard of your faith in Christ Jesus, and of the love which ye have to all the saints,

Colossians 1:3, 4

For, brethren, ye have been called unto liberty; only use not liberty for an occasion to the flesh, but by love serve one another.

For all the law is fulfilled in one word, even in this; Thou shalt love thy neighbour as thyself.

Galatians 5:13, 14

The fruit of the righteous is a tree of life; and he that winneth souls is wise.

Proverbs 11:30

And Jesus came and spake unto them, saying, All power is given unto me in heaven and in earth.

Go ye therefore, and teach all nations, baptizing them in the name of the Father, and of the Son, and of the Holy Ghost:

Teaching them to observe all things whatsoever I have commanded you: and, lo, I am with you alway, even unto the end of the world. Amen

Matthew 28:18-20

And he said unto them, Go ye into all the world, and preach the gospel to every creature.

Mark 16:15

A fruitful life for your family

Praise ye the Lord. Blessed is the man that feareth the Lord that delighteth greatly in his commandments.

His seed shall be mighty upon earth: the generation of the upright shall be blessed.

Wealth and riches shall be in his house: and his righteousness endureth for ever.

Psalms 112:1-3

That our sons may be as plants grown up in their youth; that our daughters may be as corner stones, polished after the similitude of a palace:

That our garners may be full, affording all manner of store: that our sheep may bring forth thousands and ten thousands in our streets:

That our oxen may be strong to labour; that there be no breaking in, nor going out; that there be no complaining in our streets.

Happy is that people, that is in such a case: yea, happy is that people, whose God is the Lord.

Psalms 144:12-15

The wicked desireth the net of evil men: but the root of the righteous yieldeth fruit.

The wicked is snared by the transgression of his lips: but the just shall come out of trouble.

A man shall be satisfied with good by the fruit of his mouth: and the recompence of a man's hands shall be rendered unto him.

Proverbs 12:12-14

And I will rejoice in Jerusalem, and joy in my people: and the voice of weeping shall be no more heard in her, nor the voice of crying.

There shall be no more thence an infant of days, nor an old man that hath not filled his days: for the child shall die an hundred years old; but the sinner being an hundred years old shall be accursed.

And they shall build houses, and inhabit them; and they shall plant vineyards, and eat the fruit of them.

They shall not build, and another inhabit; they shall not plant, and another eat: for as the days of a tree are the days of my people, and mine elect shall long enjoy the work of their hands.

They shall not labour in vain, nor bring forth for trouble; for they are the seed of the blessed of the Lord, and their offspring with them.

And it shall come to pass, that before they call, I will answer; and while are yet speaking, I will hear.

Isaiah 65:19-24

For God will save Zion, and will build the cities of Judah: that they may dwell there, and have it in possession.

The seed also of his servants shall inherit it: and they that love his name shall dwell therein.

Psalms 69:35, 36

For the Lord God is a sun and shield: the Lord will give grace and glory: no good thing will he withhold from them that walk uprightly.

O Lord of hosts, blessed is the man that trusteth in thee.

Psalms 84:11, 12

Let thy work appear unto thy servants, and thy glory unto their children.

And let the beauty of the Lord our God be upon us: and establish thou the work of our hands upon us; yea, the work of our hands establish thou it.

Psalms 90:16, 17

Behold, I will bring them from the north country, and gather them from the coasts of the earth, and with them the blind and the lame, the woman with child and her that travaileth with child together: a great company shall return thither.

They shall come with weeping, and with supplications will I lead them: I will cause them to walk by the rivers of waters in a straight way, wherein they shall not stumble: for I am a father to Israel, and Ephraim is my firstborn.

Hear the word of the Lord, O ye nations, and declare it in the isles afar off, and say, He that scattered Israel will gather him, and keep him, as a shepherd doth his flock.

Jeremiah 31:8-10

And they shall teach no more every man his neighbour, and every man his brother, saying, Know the Lord: for they shall all know me, from the least of them unto the greatest of them, saith the Lord: for I will forgive their iniquity, and I wil¹ remember their sin no more.

Jeremiah 31:34

The house of the wicked shall be overthrown: but the tabernacle of the upright shall flourish.

Proverbs 14:11

And in that day will I make a covenant for them with the beasts of the field, and with the fowls of heavens, and with the creeping things of the ground: and I will break the bow and the sword and the battle out of the earth, and will make them to lie down safely.

And I will betroth thee unto me for ever; yea, I will betroth thee unto me in righteousness, and in judgment, and in lovingkindness, and in mercies.

I will even betroth thee unto me in faithfulness: and thou shalt know the Lord.

And it shall come to pass in that day, I will hear, saith the Lord, I will hear the heavens, and they shall hear the earth;

And the earth shall hear the corn, and the wine, and the oil; and they shall hear Jezreel.

And I will sow her unto me in the earth; and I will have mercy upon her that had not obtained mercy; and I will say to them which were not my people, Thou art my people; and they shall say, Thou art my God.

Hosea 2:18-23

A peaceful and more hopeful world for your children

All the ends of the world shall remember and turn unto the Lord: and all the kindreds of the nations shall worship before thee.

For the kingdom is the Lord's: and he is the governor among the nations.

All they that be fat upon earth shall eat and worship: all they that go down to the dust shall bow before him: and none can keep alive his own soul.

A seed shall serve him; it shall be accounted to the Lord for a generation.

They shall come, and shall declare his righteousness unto a people that shall be born, that he hath done this.

Psalms 22:27-31

When a man's ways please the Lord, he maketh even his enemies to be at peace with him.

Proverbs 16:7

If it be possible, as much as lieth in you, live peaceably with all men.

Dearly beloved, avenge not yourselves, but rather give place unto wrath: for it is written, Vengeance is mine; I will repay, saith the Lord.

Therefore if thine enemy hunger, feed him; if he thirst, give him drink: for in so doing thou shalt heap coals of fire on his head.

Be not overcome of evil, but overcome evil with good.

Romans 12:18-21

The mountains shall bring peace to the people, and the little hills, by righteousness.

He shall judge the poor of the people, he shall save the children of the needy, and shall break in pieces the oppressor.

They shall fear thee as long as the sun and moon endure, throughout all generations.

He shall come down like rain upon the mown grass: as showers that water the earth.

In his days shall the righteous flourish; and abundance of peace so long as the moon endureth.

He shall have dominion also from sea to sea, and from the river unto the ends of the earth.

They that dwell in the wilderness shall bow before him; and his enemies shall lick the dust.

Psalms 72:3-9

Surely his salvation is nigh them that fear him; that glory may dwell in our land.

Mercy and truth are met together; righteousness and peace have kissed each other.

Truth shall spring out of the earth; and righteousness shall look down from heaven.

Yea, the Lord shall give that which is good; and our land shall yield her increase.

Righteousness shall go before him; and shall set us in the way of his steps.

Psalms 85:9-13

For yet a little while, and the wicked shall not be: yea, thou shalt diligently consider his place, and it shall not be.

But the meek shall inherit the earth; and shall delight themselves in the abundance of peace.

The wicked plotteth against the just, and gnasheth upon him with his teeth.

The Lord shall laugh at him: for he seeth that his day is coming.

Psalms 37:10-13

O give thanks unto the Lord, for he is good: for his mercy endureth for ever.

Let the redeemed of the Lord say so, whom he hath redeemed from the hand of the enemy;

And gathered them out of the lands, from the east, and from the west, from the north, and from the south.

They wandered in the wilderness in a solitary way; they found no city to dwell in.

Hungry and thirsty, their soul fainted in them.

Then they cried unto the Lord in their trouble, and he delivered them out of their distresses.

And he led them forth by the right way, that they might go to a city of habitation.

Oh that men would praise the Lord for his goodness, and for his wonderful works to the children of men!

For he satisfieth the longing soul, and filleth the hungry soul with goodness.

Psalms 107:1-9

God Rejoices When...

Your family anticipates His return

Behold, what manner of love the Father hath bestowed upon us, that we should be called the sons of God: therefore the world knoweth us not, because it knew him not.

Beloved, now are we the sons of God, and it doth not yet appear what we shall be: but we know that when he shall appear, we shall be like him; for we shall see him as he is.

And every man that hath this hope in him purifieth himself, even as he is pure.

I John 3:1-3

For, behold, I create new heavens and a new earth: and the former shall not be remembered, nor come into mind.

But be ye glad and rejoice for ever in that which I create: for, behold, I create Jerusalem a rejoicing, and her people a joy.

And I will rejoice in Jerusalem, and joy in my people: and the voice of weeping shall be no more heard in her, nor the voice of crying.

Isaiah 65:17-19

Therefore the redeemed of the Lord shall return, and come with singing unto Zion; and everlasting joy shall be upon their head: they shall obtain gladness and joy; and sorrow and mourning shall flee away.

Isaiah 51:11

To such as keep his covenant, and to those that remember his commandments to do them.

The Lord hath prepared his throne in the heavens; and his kingdom ruleth over all.

Psalms 103:18, 19

It is good that a man should both hope and quietly wait for the salvation of the Lord.

Lamentations 3:26

For as the lightning cometh out of the east, and shineth even unto the west; so shall also the coming of the Son of man be.

For wheresoever the carcase is, there will the eagles be gathered together.

Immediately after the tribulation of those days shall the sun be darkened, and the moon shall not give her light, and the stars shall fall from heaven, and the powers of the heavens shall be shaken:

And then shall appear the sign of the Son of man in heaven: and then shall all the tribes of the earth mourn, and they shall see the Son of man coming in the clouds of heaven with power and great glory.

And he shall send his angels with a great sound of a trumpet, and they shall gather together his elect from the four winds, from the one end of heaven to the other.

Matthew 24:27-31

And there shall be signs in the sun, and in the moon, and in the stars; and upon the earth distress of nations, with perplexity; the sea and the waves roaring;

Men's hearts failing them for fear, and for looking after those things which are coming on the earth: for the powers of heaven shall be shaken.

And then shall they see the Son of man coming in a cloud with power and great glory.

And when these things begin to come to pass, then look up, and lift up your heads; for your redemption draweth nigh.

Luke 21:25-28

But the day of the Lord will come as a thief in the night; in the which the heavens shall pass away with a great noise, and the elements shall melt with fervent heat, the earth also and the works that are therein shall be burned up.

Seeing then that all these things shall be dissolved, what manner of persons ought ye to be in all holy conversation and godliness,

Looking for and hasting unto the coming of the day of God, wherein the heavens being on fire shall be dissolved, and the elements shall melt with fervent heat?

II Peter 3:10-12

He that believeth on the Son of God hath the witness in himself: he that believeth not God hath made him a liar; because he believeth not the record that God gave of his Son.

And this is the record, that God hath given to us eternal life, and this life is in his Son.

He that hath the Son hath life; and he that hath not the Son of God hath not life.

These things have I written unto you that believe on the name of the Son of God; that ye may know that ye have eternal life, and that ye may believe on the name of the Son of God.

I John 5:10-13

Which also said, Ye men of Galilee, why stand ye gazing up into heaven? this same Jesus, which is taken up from you into heaven, shall so come in like manner as ye have seen him go into heaven.

Acts 1:11

And God shall wipe away all tears from their eyes; and there shall be no more death, neither sorrow, nor crying, neither shall there be any more pain: for the former things are passed away.

Revelation 21:4

Looking for that blessed hope, and the glorious appearing of the great God and our Saviour Jesus Christ;

Titus 2:13

You dedicate your children to Him

And their seed shall be known among the Gentiles, and their offspring among the people: all that see them shall acknowledge them, that they are the seed which the Lord hath blessed.

I will greatly rejoice in the Lord, my soul shall be joyful in my God; for he hath clothed me with the garments of salvation, he hath covered me with the robe of righteousness, as a bridegroom decketh himself with ornaments, and as a bride adorneth herself with her jewels.

For as the earth bringeth forth her bud, and as the garden causeth the things that are sown in it to spring forth; so the Lord God will cause righteousness and praise to spring forth before all the nations.

Isaiah 61:9-11

For as many of you as have been baptized into Christ have put on Christ.

There is neither Jew nor Greek, there is neither bond nor free, there is neither male nor female: for ye are all one in Christ Jesus.

And if ye be Christ's, then are ye Abraham's seed, and heirs according to the promise.

Galatians 3:27-29

And when eight days were accomplished for the circumcising of the child, his name was called JESUS, which was so named of the angel before he was conceived in the womb.

And when the days of her purification according to the law of Moses were accomplished, they brought him to Jerusalem, to present him to the Lord;

(As it is written in the law of the Lord, Every male that openeth the womb shall be called holy to the Lord;)

And to offer a sacrifice according to that which is said in the law of the Lord, A pair of turtledoves, or two young pigeons.

Luke 2:21-24

For I will pour water upon him that is thirsty, and floods upon the dry ground: I will pour my spirit upon thy seed, and my blessing upon thine offspring:

Isaiah 44:3

Who hath wrought and done it, calling the generations from the beginning? I the Lord, the first, and with the last; I am he.

Isaiah 41:4

But now, O Lord, thou art our father; we are the clay, and thou our potter; and we all are the work of thy hand.

Isaiah 64:8

And she was in bitterness of soul, and prayed unto the Lord, and wept sore.

And she vowed a vow, and said, O Lord of hosts, if thou wilt indeed look on the affliction of thine handmaid, and remember me, and not forget thine handmaid, but wilt give unto thine handmaid a man child, then I will give him unto the Lord all the days of his life, and there shall no razor come upon his head.

Wherefore it came to pass, when the time was come about after Hannah had conceived, that she bare a son, and called his name Samuel, saying, Because I have asked him of the Lord.

And the man Elkanah, and all his house, went up to offer unto the Lord the yearly sacrifice, and his vow.

But Hannah went not up; for she said unto her husband, I will not go up until the child be weaned, and then I will bring him, that he may appear before the Lord, and there abide for ever.

And Elkanah her husband said unto her, Do what seemeth thee good; tarry until thou have weaned him; only the Lord establish his word. So the woman abode, and gave her son suck until she weaned him.

And she said, Oh my lord, as thy soul liveth, my lord, I am the woman that stood by thee here, praying unto the Lord.

For this child I prayed; and the Lord hath given me my petition which I asked of him:

Therefore also I have lent him to the Lord; as long as he liveth he shall be lent to the Lord. And he worshipped the Lord there.

I Samuel 1:10, 11, 20-23, 26-28

But Samuel ministered before the Lord, being a child, girded with a linen ephod.

Moreover his mother made him a little coat and bought it to him from year to year, when she came up with her husband to offer the yearly sacrifice.

And Eli blessed Elkanah and his wife, and said, The Lord give thee seed of this woman for the loan which is lent to the Lord. And they went unto their own home.

I Samuel 2:18-20

And now, little children, abide in him; that, when he shall appear, we may have confidence, and not be ashamed before him at his coming.

I John 2:28

A little one shall become a thousand, and a small one a strong nation: I the Lord will hasten it in his time.

Isaiah 60:22

You trust Him and wait for His answers

I waited patiently for the Lord; and he inclined unto me, and heard my cry.

Psalms 40:1

My soul, wait thou only upon God; for my expectation is from him.

He only is my rock and my salvation: he is my defence; I shall not be moved.

In God is my salvation and my glory: the rock of my strength, and my refuge, is in God.

Trust in him at all times; ye people, pour out your heart before him: God is a refuge for us. Selah.

Psalms 62:5-8

Let them all be confounded and turned back that hate Zion.

Let them be as the grass upon the house tops, which withereth afore it groweth up:

Wherewith the mower filleth not his hand; nor he that bindeth sheaves his bosom.

Neither do they which go by say, The blessing of the Lord be upon you: we bless you in the name of the Lord.

Psalms 129:5-8

Turn again, my daughters, go your way; for I am too old to have an husband. If I should say, I have hope, if I should have an husband also to night, and should also bear sons;

Would ye tarry for them till they were grown? would ye stay for them from having husbands? nay, my daughters; for it grieveth me much for your sakes that the hand of the Lord is gone out against me.

And Ruth said, Entreat me not to leave thee, or to return from following after thee: for whither thou goest, I will go; and where thou lodgest, I will lodge: thy people shall be my people, and thy God my God:

Where thou diest, will I die, and there will I be buried: the Lord do so to me, and more also, if ought but death part thee and me.

When she saw that she was stedfastly minded to go with her then she left speaking unto her.

So Boaz took Ruth, and she was his wife: and when he went in unto her, the Lord gave her conception, and she bare a son.

And the women said unto Naomi, Blessed be the Lord, which hath not left thee this day without a kinsman, that his name may be famous in Israel.

And he shall be unto thee a restorer of thy life, and a nourisher of thine old age: for thy daughter in law, which loveth thee, which is better to thee than seven sons, hath borne him.

And Naomi took the child, and laid it in her bosom, and became nurse unto it.

And the women her neighbours gave it a name, saying, There is a son born to Naomi; and they called his name Obed: he is the father of Jesse, the father of David.

Ruth 1:12, 13, 16-18 and 4:13-17

Every word of God is pure: he is a shield unto them that put their trust in him.

Proverbs 30:5

But they that wait upon the Lord shall renew their strength; they shall mount up with wings as eagles; they shall run, and not be weary; and they shall walk, and not faint.

Isaiah 40:31

I am the Lord, and there is none else, there is no God beside me: I girded thee, though thou hast not known me:

That they may know from the rising of the sun, and from the west, that there is none beside me. I am the Lord, and there is none else.

Isaiah 45:5, 6

For since the beginning of the world men have not heard, nor perceived by the ear, neither hath the eye seen, O God, beside thee, what he hath prepared for him that waiteth for him.

Isaiah 64:4

And ye shall eat in plenty, and be satisfied, and praise the name of the Lord your God, that hath dealt wondrously with you: and my people shall never be ashamed.

Joel 2:26

The Lord thy God in the midst of thee is mighty; he will save, he will rejoice over thee with joy; he will rest in his love, he will joy over thee with singing.

Zephaniah 3:17

That ye be not slothful, but followers of them who through faith and patience inherit the promises.

Hebrews 6:12

As unknown, and yet well known; as dying, and, behold, we live; as chastened, and not killed;

As sorrowful, yet alway rejoicing; as poor, yet making many rich; as having nothing, and yet possessing all things.

II Corinthians 6:9, 10

For verily I say unto you, Till heaven and earth pass, one jot or one tittle shall in no wise pass from the law, till all be fulfilled.

Whosoever therefore shall break one of these least commandments, and shall teach men so, he shall be called the least in the kingdom of heaven: but whosoever shall do and teach them, the same shall be called great in the kingdom of heaven.

For I say unto you, That except your righteousness shall exceed the righteousness of the scribes and Pharisees, ye shall in no case enter into the kingdom of heaven.

Matthew 5:18-20

Do not err, my beloved brethren.

Every good gift and every perfect gift is from above, and cometh down from the Father of lights, with whom is no variableness, neither shadow of turning.

James 1:16, 17

Jesus Christ the same yesterday, and to day, and for ever.

Hebrews 13:8

You teach your children to show mercy to others

And all his sons and all his daughters rose up to comfort him;

Genesis 37:35a

Therefore the Lord hath recompensed me according to my righteousness; according to my cleanness in his eye sight.

With the merciful thou wilt shew thyself merciful, and with the upright man thou wilt shew thyself upright.

II Samuel 22:25, 26

And if thou draw out thy soul to the hungry, and satisfy the afflicted soul; then shall thy light rise in obscurity, and thy darkness be as the noon day:

And the Lord shall guide thee continually, and satisfy thy soul in drought, and make fat thy bones: and thou shalt be like a watered garden, and like a spring of water, whose waters fail not.

And they that shall be of thee shall build the old waste places: thou shalt raise up the foundations of many generations; and thou shalt be called, The repairer of the breach, The restorer of paths to dwell in.

Isaiah 58:10-12

But love ye your enemies, and do good, and lend, hoping for nothing again; and your reward shall be great, and ye shall be the children of the Highest: for he is kind unto the unthankful and to the evil.

Be ye therefore merciful, as your Father also is merciful.

Judge not, and ye shall not be judge: condemn not, and ye shall not be condemned: forgive, and ye shall be forgiven:

Give, and it shall be given unto you; good measure, pressed down, and shaken together, and running over, shall men give into your bosom. For with the same measure that ye mete withal it shall be measured to you again.

Luke 6:35-38

And let us not be weary in well doing: for in due season we shall reap, if we faint not.

As we have therefore opportunity, let us do good unto all men, especially unto them who are of the household of faith.

Galatians 6:9, 10

And her neighbours and her cousins heard how the Lord had shewed great mercy upon her; and they rejoiced with her.

Luke 1:58

Bear ye one another's burdens, and so fulfil the law of Christ.

Galatians 6:2

God's Dynamic Examples Of Fathers Who Cared...

Abraham

Now the Lord had said unto Abram, Get thee out of thy country, and from thy kindred, and from thy father's house, unto a land that I will shew thee:

And I will make of thee a great nation, and I will bless thee, and make thy name great; and thou shalt be a blessing:

And I will bless them that bless thee, and curse him that curseth thee: and in thee shall all families of the earth be blessed.

Genesis 12:1-3

And the Lord said unto Abram, after that Lot was separated from him, Lift up now thine eyes, and look from the place where thou art northward, and southward, and eastward, and westward:

For all the land which thou seest, to thee will I give it, and to thy seed for ever.

And I will make thy seed as the dust of the earth: so that if a man can number the dust of the earth, then shall thy seed also be numbered.

Genesis 13:14-16

After these things the word of the Lord came unto Abram in a vision, saying, Fear not, Abram: I am thy shield, and thy exceeding great reward.

And Abram said, Lord God, what wilt thou give me, seeing I go childless, and the steward of my house is this Eliezer of Damascus?

And Abram said, Behold, to me thou hast given no seed: and, lo, one born in my house is mine heir.

And, behold, the word of the Lord came unto him, saying, This shall not be thine heir; but he that shall come forth out of thine own bowels shall be thine heir.

And he brought him forth abroad, and said, Look now toward heaven, and tell the stars, if thou be able to number them: and he said unto him, So shall thy seed be.

And he believed in the Lord; and he counted it to him for righteousness.

Genesis 15:1-6

And when Abram was ninety years old and nine, the Lord appeared to Abram, and said unto him, I am the Almighty God; walk before me, and be thou perfect.

And I will make my covenant between me and thee, and will multiply thee exceedingly.

And Abram fell on his face: and God talked with him, saying,

As for me, behold, my covenant is with thee, and thou shalt be a father of many nations.

Neither shall thy name any more be called Abram, but thy name shall be Abraham; for a father of many nations have I made thee.

Genesis 17:1-5

For it is written, that Abraham had two sons, the one by a bondmaid, the other by a freewoman.

But he who was of the bondwoman was born after the flesh; but he of the freewoman was by promise.

Which things are an allegory: for these are the two covenants; the one from the mount Sinai, which gendereth to bondage, which is Agar.

Galatians 4:22-24

And Jesus said unto him, This day is salvation come to this house, forsomuch as he also is a son of Abraham.

Luke 19:9

He opened the rock, and the waters gushed out; they ran in the dry places like a river.

For he remembered his holy promise, and Abraham his servant.

And he brought forth his people with joy, and his chosen with gladness:

And gave them the lands of the heathen: and they inherited the labour of the people;

That they might observe his statutes, and keep his laws. Praise ye the Lord.

Psalms 105:41-45

Know ye therefore that they which are of faith, the same are the children of Abraham.

And the scripture, foreseeing that God would justify the heathen through faith, preached before the gospel unto Abraham, saying, In thee shall all nations be blessed.

So then they which be of faith are blessed with faithful Abraham.

Galatians 3:7-9

And the Lord visited Sarah as he had said, and the Lord did unto Sarah as he had spoken.

For Sarah conceived, and bare Abraham a son in his old age, at the set time of which God had spoken to him.

And Abraham called the name of his son that was born unto him, whom Sarah bare to him, Isaac.

And Abraham circumcised his son Isaac being eight days old, as God had commanded him.

An Abraham was an hundred years old, when his son Isaac was born unto him.

And Sarah said, God hath made me to laugh, so that all that hear will laugh with me.

And she said, Who would have said unto Abraham, that Sarah should have given children suck? for I have born him a son in his old age.

And the child grew, and was weaned: and Abraham made a great feast the same day that Isaac was weaned.

Genesis 21: 1-8

Jacob

Sing aloud unto God our strength: make a joyful noise unto the God of Jacob.

Take a psalm, and bring hither the timbrel, the pleasant harp with the psaltery.

Blow up the trumpet in the new moon, in the time appointed, on our solemn feast day.

For this was a statute for Israel, and a law of the God of Jacob.

I am the Lord thy God, which brought thee out of the land of Egypt: open thy mouth wide, and I will fill it.

Psalms 81:1-4, 10

Then the Lord awaked as one out of sleep, and like a mighty man that shouteth by reason of wine.

And he smote his enemies in the hinder parts: he put them to a perpetual reproach.

Moreover he refused the tabernacle of Joseph, and chose not the tribe of Ephraim:

But chose the tribe of Judah, the mount Zion which he loved.

And he built his sanctuary like high palaces, like the earth which he hath established for ever.

He chose David also his servant, and took him from the sheepfolds:

From following the ewes great with young he brought him to feed Jacob his people, and Israel his inheritance.

So he fed them according to the integrity of his heart; and guided them by the skilfulness of his hands.

Psalms 78:65-72

And Jacob was left alone; and there wrestled a man with him until the breaking of the day.

And when he saw that he prevailed not against him, he touched the hollow of his thigh; and the hollow of Jacob's thigh was out of joint, as he wrestled with him.

And he said, Let me go, for the day breaketh. And he said, I will not let thee go, except thou bless me.

And he said unto him, What is thy name? And he said, Jacob.

And he said, Thy name shall be called no more Jacob, but Israel: for as a prince hast thou power with God and with men, and hast prevailed.

And Jacob asked him, and said, Tell me, I pray thee, thy name. And he said, Wherefore is it that thou dost ask after my name? And he blessed him there.

And Jacob called the name of the place Peniel: for I have seen God face to face, and my life is preserved.

Genesis 32:24-30

And God said unto Jacob, Arise, go up to Bethel, and dwell there: and make there an altar unto God, that appeared unto thee when thou fleddest from the face of Esau thy brother.

Then Jacob said unto his household, and to all that were with him, Put away the strange gods that are among you, and be clean, and change your garments:

And let us arise, and go up to Bethel; and I will make there an altar unto God, who answered me in the day of my distress, and was with me in the way which I went.

Genesis 35:1-3

And God said unto him, Thy name is Jacob: thy name shall not be called any more Jacob, but Israel shall be thy name: and he called his name Israel.

And God said unto him, I am God Almighty: be fruitful and multiply; a nation and a company of nations shall be of thee, and kings shall come out of thy loins;

Genesis 35:10, 11

And they sent the coat of many colours, and they brought it to their father; and said, This have we found: know now whether it be thy son's coat or no.

And he knew it, and said, It is my son's coat; an evil beast hath devoured him; Joseph is without doubt rent in pieces.

And Jacob rent his clothes, and put sackcloth upon his loins, and mourned for his son many days.

And all his sons and all his daughters rose up to comfort him; but he refused to be comforted; and he said, For I will go down into the grave unto my son mourning. Thus his father wept for him.

Genesis 37:32-35

Now when Jacob saw that there was corn in Egypt, Jacob said unto his sons, Why do ye look one upon another?

And he said, Behold I have heard that there is corn in Egypt: get you down thither, and buy for us from thence; that we may live, and not die.

Genesis 42:1, 2

And they told him all the words of Joseph, which he had said unto them: and when he saw the wagons which Joseph had sent to carry him, the spirit of Jacob their father revived:

And Israel said, It is enough; Joseph my son is yet alive: I will go and see him before I die.

Genesis 45:27, 28

Joseph — Jacob's son

And unto Joseph were born two sons before the years of famine came, which Asenath the daughter of Potipherah priest of On bare unto him.

And Joseph called the name of the firstborn Manasseh: For God, said he, hath made me forget all my toil, and all my father's house.

And the name of the second called he Ephraim: For God hath caused me to be fruitful in the land of my affliction.

And the seven years of plenteousness, that was in the land of Egypt, were ended.

And the seven years of dearth began to come, according as Joseph had said: and the dearth was in all lands; but in all the land of Egypt there was bread.

And when all the land of Egypt was famished, the people cried to Pharaoh for bread: and Pharoah said unto all the Egyptians, Go unto Joseph; what he saith to you, do.

And the famine was over all the face of the earth: And Joseph opened all the storehouses, and sold unto the Egyptians; and the famine waxed sore in the land of Egypt.

And all countries came into Egypt to Joseph for to buy corn; because that the famine was so sore in all lands.

Genesis 41:50-57

Then Joseph could not refrain himself before all them that stood by him; and he cried, Cause every man to go out from me. And there stood no man with him, while Joseph made himself known unto his brethren.

And he wept aloud: and the Egyptians and the house of Pharaoh heard.

And Joseph said unto his brethren, I am Joseph; doth my father yet live? And his brethren could not answer him; for they were troubled at his presence.

And Joseph said unto his brethren, Come near to me, I pray you. And they came near. And he said, I am Joseph your brother, whom ye sold into Egypt.

Now therefore be not grieved, nor angry with yourselves, that ye sold me hither: for God did send me before you to preserve life.

For these two years hath the famine been in the land: and yet there are five years, in the which there shall neither be earing nor harvest.

And God sent me before you to preserve you a posterity in the earth, and to save your lives by a great deliverance.

So now it was not you that sent me hither, but God: and he hath made me a father to Pharaoh, and lord of all his house, and a ruler throughout all the land of Egypt.

Haste ye, and go up to my father, and say unto him, Thus saith thy son Joseph, God hath made me lord of all Egypt: come down unto me, tarry not:

And thou shalt dwell in the land of Goshen, and thou shalt be near unto me, thou, and thy children, and thy children's children, and thy flocks, and thy herds, and all that thou hast.

Genesis 45:1-10

An Joseph nourished his father, and his brethren, and all his father's household, with bread, according to their families.

Genesis 47:12

And Israel beheld Joseph's sons, and said, Who are these?

And Joseph said unto his father, They are my sons, whom God hath given me in this place. And he said, Bring them, I pray thee, unto me, and I will bless them.

Now the eyes of Israel were dim for age, so that he could not see. And he brought them near unto him; and he kissed them, and embraced them.

Genesis 48:8-10

And Joseph fell upon his father's face, and wept upon him, and kissed him.

Genesis 50:1

David

Arise, O Lord, into thy rest; thou, and the ark of thy strength.

Let thy priests be clothed with righteousness; and let thy saints shout for joy.

For thy servant David's sake turn not away the face of thine anointed.

The Lord hath sworn in truth unto David; he will not turn from it; Of the fruit of thy body will I set upon thy throne.

If thy children will keep my covenant and my testimony that I shall teach them, their children shall also sit upon thy throne for evermore.

For the Lord hath chosen Zion; he hath desired it for his habitation.

This is my rest for ever: here will I dwell; for I have desired it.

I will abundantly bless her provision: I will satisfy her poor with bread.

I will also clothe her priests with salvation: and her saints shall shout aloud for joy.

There will I make the horn of David to bud: I have ordained a lamp for mine anointed.

His enemies will I cloth with shame: but upon himself shall his crown flourish.

Psalms 132:8-18

Incline your ear, and come unto me: hear, and your soul shall live; and I will make an everlasting covenant with you, even the sure mercies of David.

Behold, I have given him for a witness to the people, a leader and commander to the people.
Isaiah 55:3, 4

And David spake unto the Lord the words of this song in the day that the Lord had delivered him out of the hand of all his enemies, and out of the hand of Saul:

For thou art my lamp, O Lord: and the Lord will lighten my darkness.

For by thee I have run through a troop: by my God have I leaped over a wall.

As for God, his way is perfect; the word of the Lord is tried: he is a buckler to all them that trust in him.

For who is God, save the Lord? and who is a rock, save our God?

God is my strength and power: and he maketh my way perfect.

He maketh my feet like hinds' feet: and setteth me upon my high places.

He teacheth my hands to war; so that a bow of steel is broken by mine arms.

Thou hast also given me the shield of thy salvation: and thy gentleness hath made me great.
II Samuel 22:1, 29-36

For David speaketh concerning him, I foresaw the Lord always before my face, for he is on my right hand, that I should not be moved:
Acts 2:25

Even as David also describeth the blessedness of the man, unto whom God imputeth righteousness without works,

Saying, Blessed are they whose iniquities are forgiven, and whose sins are covered.

Blessed is the man to whom the Lord will not impute sin.

Romans 4:6-8

And David said to Solomon his son, Be strong and of good courage, and do it: fear not, nor be dismayed: for the Lord God, even my God, will be with thee; he will not fail thee, nor forsake thee, until thou hast finished all the work for the service of the house of the Lord.

I Chronicles 28:20

And as for thee, if thou wilt walk before me, as David thy father walked, and do according to all that I have commanded thee, and shalt observe my statutes and my judgments;

Then will I stablish the throne of thy kingdom, according as I have covenanted with David thy father, saying, There shall not fail thee a man to be ruler in Israel.

II Chronicles 7:17, 18

Manoah — Samson's father

And the children of Israel did evil again in the sight of the Lord; and the Lord delivered them into the hand of the Philistines forty years.

And there was a certain man of Zorah, of the family of the Danites, whose name was Manoah; and his wife was barren, and bare not.

And the angel of the Lord appeared unto the woman, and said unto her, Behold now, thou art barren, and bearest not: but thou shalt conceive, and bear a son.

Now therefore beware, I pray thee, and drink not wine nor strong drink, and eat not any unclean thing:

For, lo, thou shalt conceive, and bear a son; and no razor shall come on his head: for the child shall be a Nazarite unto God from the womb: and he shall begin to deliver Israel out of the hand of the Philistines.,

Then the woman came and told her husband, saying, A man of God came unto me, and his countenance was like the countenance of an angel of God, very terrible: but I asked him not whence he was, neither told he me his name:

But he said unto me, Behold, thou shalt conceive, and bear a son; and now drink no wine nor strong drink, neither eat any unclean thing: for the child shall be a Nazarite to God from the womb to the day of his death.

Judges 13:1-7

And the woman bare a son, and called his name Samson: and the child grew, and the Lord blessed him.

And the Spirit of the Lord began to move him at times in the camp of Dan between Zorah and Eshtaol.

Judges 13:24, 25

Zacharias — John's father

There was in the days of Herod, the king of Judaea, a certain priest named Zacharias, of the course of Abia: and his wife was of the daughters of Aaron, and her name was Elisabeth.

And they were both righteous before God, walking in all the commandments and ordinances of the Lord blameless.

And they had no child, because that Elisabeth was barren, and they both were now well stricken in years.

And it came to pass, that while he executed the priest's office before God in the order of his course.

According to the custom of the priest's office, his lot was to burn incense when he went into the temple of the Lord.

And the whole multitude of the people were praying without at the time of incense.

And there appeared unto him an angel of the Lord standing on the right side of the altar of incense.

And when Zacharias saw him, he was troubled, and fear fell upon him.

But the angel said unto him. Fear not, Zacharias: for thy prayer is heard; and thy wife Elisabeth shall bear thee a son, and thou shalt call his name John.

And thou shalt have joy and gladness; and many shall rejoice at his birth.

For he shall be great in the sight of the Lord, and shall drink neither wine nor strong drink; and he shall be filled with the Holy Ghost, even from his mother's womb.

Luke 1:5-15

Now Elisabeth's full time came that she should be delivered; and she brought forth a son.

And her neighbours and her cousins heard how the Lord had shewed great mercy upon her; and they rejoiced with her.

And it came to pass, that on the eight day they came to circumcise the child; and they called him Zacharias, after the name of his father.

And his mother answered and said, Not so; but he shall be called John.

And they said unto her, There is none of thy kindred that is called by this name.

And they made signs to his father, how he would have him called.

And he asked for a writing table, and wrote, saying, His name is John. And they marvelled all.

And his mouth was opened immediately, and his tongue loosed and he spake, and praised God.

And his father Zacharias was filled with the Holy Ghost, and prophesied, saying,

Blessed be the Lord God of Israel; for he hath visited and redeemed his people,

And the child grew, and waxed strong in spirit, and was in the deserts til the day of his shewing unto Israel.

Luke 1:57-64, 67, 68, 80

Noah

And he called his name Noah, saying, This same shall comfort us concerning our work and toil of our hands, because of the ground which the Lord hath cursed.

Genesis 5:29

And the Lord said, I will destroy man whom I have created from the face of the earth; both man, and beast, and the creeping thing, and the fowls of the air; for it repenteth me that I have made them.

But Noah found grace in the eyes of the Lord.

These are the generations of Noah: Noah was a just man and perfect in his generations, and Noah walked with God.

And Noah begat three sons, Shem, Ham, and Japheth.

Genesis 6:7-10

And the Lord said unto Noah, Come thou and all thy house into the ark; for thee have I seen righteous before me in this generation.

And Noah went in, and his sons, and his wife, and his sons' wives with him, into the ark, because of the waters of the flood

Genesis 7:1, 7

And every living substance was destroyed which was upon the face of the ground, both man, and cattle, and the creeping things, and the fowl of the heaven; and they were destroyed from the earth: and Noah only remained alive, and they that were with him in the ark.

And the waters prevailed upon the earth an hundred and fifty days.

And God remembered Noah, and every living thing, and all the cattle that was with him in the ark: and God made a wind to pass over the earth, and the waters assuaged.

Genesis 7:23-8:1

And God spake unto Noah, saying,

Go forth of the ark, thou, and thy wife, and thy sons, and thy sons' wives with thee.

Genesis 8:15, 16

And God blessed Noah and his sons, and said unto them, Be fruitful and multiply, and replenish the earth.

And God spake unto Noah, and to his sons with him, saying,

And I, behold, I establish my covenant with you, and with your seed after you;

Genesis 9:1, 8, 9

But without faith it is impossible to please him: for he that cometh to God must believe that he is, and that he is a rewarder of them that diligently seek him.

By faith Noah, being warned of God of things not seen as yet, moved with fear, prepared an ark to the saving of his house; by the which he condemned the world, and became heir of the righteousness which is by faith.

Hebrews 11:6, 7

Joseph, Mary's husband

Now the birth of Jesus Christ was on this wise: When as his mother Mary was espoused to Joseph, before they came together, she was found with child of the Holy Ghost.

Then Joseph her husband, being a just man, and not willing to make her a public example, was minded to put her away privily.

But while he thought on these things, behold, the angel of the Lord appeared unto him in a dream, saying, Joseph, thou son of David, fear not to take unto thee Mary thy wife: for that which is conceived in her is of the Holy Ghost.

And she shall bring forth a son and thou shalt call his name JESUS: for he shall save his people from their sins.

Now all this was done, that it might be fulfilled which was spoken of the Lord by the prophet, saying,

Behold, a virgin shall be with child, and shall bring forth a son, and they shall call his name Emmanuel, which being interpreted is, God with us.

Then Joseph being raised from sleep did as the angel of the Lord had bidden him, and took unto him his wife:

And knew her not till she had brought forth her firstborn son: and he called his name JESUS.

Matthew 1:18-25

And when they were departed, behold, the angel of the Lord appeareth to Joseph in a dream, saying, Arise, and take the young child and his mother, and flee into Egypt, and be thou there until I bring thee word: for Herod will seek the young child to destroy him.

When he arose, he took the young child and his mother by night, and departed into Egypt:

But when Herod was dead, behold, an angel of the Lord appeareth in a dream to Joseph in Egypt,

Saying, Arise, and take the young child and his mother, and go into the land of Israel: for they are dead which sought the young child's life.

And he arose, and took the young child and his mother, and came into the land of Israel.

Matthew 2:13, 14, 19-21